COMING OUT
It Only Took Fifty Years

COMING OUT
It Only Took Fifty Years

Janis E. Mills

Desert Palm Press

Coming Out – It Only Took Fifty Year

By Janis E. Mills

©2021 Janis E. Mills

ISBN: (book) 9781954213173
ISBN (epub): 9781954213180

This book is memoir. It reflects the author's present recollections of experiences over time. Some names and characteristics have been changed, some events have been compressed, and some dialogue has been recreated.

For permission requests, write to the publisher at lee@desertpalmpress.com or "Attention: Permissions Coordinator," at

Desert Palm Press
1961 Main Street, Suite 220
Watsonville, California 95076
www.desertpalmpress.com

Editor: Kaycee Hawn
Cover Design: Michelle Broduer eeboxWORX
Cover Photo: Sherry Surratt

Printed in the United States of America
First Edition September 2021

Table of Contents

PROLOGUE

WHEN I BEGAN READING Michelle Obama's *Becoming*, her preface began with. "When I was a kid, my aspirations were simple." As I read more of her childhood thoughts–a home, a family, security–I kept thinking, *that's me*.

I wanted six kids and a house like the one I grew up in, large and red brick with a big yard, and I also wanted a horse or two. A husband was considered, in an offhand way, but he would have to be someone like Rock Hudson or Tab Hunter. They were both very handsome movie stars, one blond and one mahogany haired. Interestingly, they were both gay. I had no idea at the time but even early on, my choice in men gravitated toward those who were unavailable. I would soon learn that I was also unavailable to them. I liked girls.

So far in my life, I've been a daughter and a sister, a PhD-holding educator and school administrator, a runner and fitness enthusiast, a student of seven musical instruments (not good at any), a self-taught cook and gardener, a mentor/leadership coach, a wife. I am also a lesbian who came of age before the flourishing LGBTQ movement, unable to be true to my family, friends, and colleagues, or maybe even to myself. That lifestyle was illegal in some states and viewed as abnormal by many, even in my own family.

Coming Out: It Only Took Fifty Years chronicles the life of a girl who knew she was gay at age eight (I had a huge crush on my music teacher) and how she struggled through the lies, the triple-life playing a straight daughter, conservative educator, gay lover by night–and finally the redemption.

I was born into a devout Methodist family in the small town of Level Green, in Western Pennsylvania. Dad a welder, Mum a nurse, one sister and one brother, both heterosexual. Staying there until I graduated from college meant living a charade. Since I wanted to remain the dutiful daughter and avoid hurting the parents I loved deeply, my girlfriend gallivants were my own secrets, a source of joy for me, though deemed a dirty secret to mainstream society. My book, written after decades of hiding, is a prescriptive path meant to empower those who are gay to celebrate their truth–with loved ones and with the world, no matter their age.

My mother carried memories of tragic family deaths and a possible lesbian relationship of her own while she perfectly performed every duty of a wife, mother, and nurse. My father was more of a vagabond from a free-wheeling life, raised by a band of circus performers. His mother walked the slack wire with her family's acrobatic troupe and his father was the leader of the circus band. Dad unleashed me to be whatever I wanted to be–likely knowing intuitively that I was not a girly girl. He shot baskets with me and taught me how to golf.

This book documents my struggle to share my true self with the people I loved most while shielding them from that truth. God forbid they would have to go to church with their Level Green friends who knew they had a lesbian daughter. How ridiculous and sad those years of deceit seem today as gay pride is celebrated worldwide by gays and non-gays alike. Several opportunities to come out to my parents presented themselves over the years, but I always took the coward's way out.

Adrienne Brodeur, author of *Wild Game,* wrote that her book is "a courageous act of radical, candid self-reflection and truth-telling." I can describe writing about my life using the same words. It has not been an easy book to write because I am not proud of some of the stories I will share of weakness and deceit. Today, I tell the truth proudly and am proud of how brave I have become.

My goal in sharing my journey of pain and resilience and ultimate joy by marrying my bride, Lori, is to give others in my past situation the courage and strength to celebrate who they are and not hide. My hope is that my story, that entwines both pain and humor, will help families understand and support what some of their friends and relatives might be struggling with. Those families might also learn how they can help.

I know my mother's fears and prayers coincided with killings, laws, and bigotry against gays. There were no gay pride parades and there was no presidential candidate kissing his husband in front of millions. The culture of the fifties and sixties, when I was growing up, contributed to people's struggles with homosexuality. What I learned and what I loathed was set against the backdrop of the times and it was not easy.

The challenges in my life gave me enduring drive and tenacity. I have learned never to let my past define me because it was just a lesson, not a life sentence. This book is also my way of paying homage to those who guided me and inspired me. Most importantly, every story of each person that has added to the complicated mosaic that comprises seventy years is true. Stories are life, life is stories.

The motivation for writing my memoir has layered purposes. One is to share my mother's life experiences and how they affected and taught me. It is also to tell my side of the story–hiding my truth, how what others said affected me, building strength, staying away from my family, trying to blaze a trail in education. I try to grasp why people behaved the way they did and what their actions or words actually meant.

May my journey release others to be true to their own selves. I was not, and I learned the hard way. So, "Come out, come out, wherever you are!" We all have the right to love who we love, openly, with authenticity. We only get this one life.

Janis E. Mills

chapter one

MY HIDDEN HEART

SIXTY-TWO YEARS AGO, WHILE outside playing with the neighborhood kids, one of them called someone else a queer. I entered our kitchen, where my mother's hands were covered in a sticky paste of raw egg, flour, and bread crumbs as she prepared her signature dish, City Chicken, consisting of cubes of meat placed on a wooden skewer. I blurted out my urgent question, "What is a queer?" Without interrupting her elaborate construction, she replied, "That is when a boy likes only boys or a girl likes only girls." I wish I had said, "That's me!" At the age of eight, I knew I was gay...but I could not say those words.

Like a light switch toggling on and off, with lightning speed, my thoughts flipped back and forth from *that's not so bad* to *how am I going to explain to my mother that I am one of the queers she is talking about?* It was clear when the neighborhood boy said the word queer that he meant it in an evil way. That, and my mother's abrupt dismissal, made me feel like being queer was a bad thing, abnormal. Having the respect of a child for my mother, the person I loved more than anyone in the world, I believed that I needed to keep the secret to myself. In those times of cultural homophobia and being raised in a faithful Methodist home, it would have been considered a dirty secret.

Me at eight years old.

Now I am a seventy-year-old woman married to a woman. It took decades to get to this place of truth, though at least I did arrive. During the fifty-four years between that kitchen conversation and my wedding, there were many hard passages to navigate and lessons to learn before I would be prepared for marriage.

Since gays were not allowed to marry while I was coming of age, I didn't think much about any relationship lasting for the rest of my life. I viewed gay life as a series of lovers and partners. I presumed the last relationship in the string would be the one to continue until death, but that it wouldn't include the vow of 'til death do us part.' Neither marriage nor children were in the picture, legally, for me, so I did not think about a forever relationship the same way straight people did.

Then came Lori. I met the tall, beautiful, green-eyed blonde in Rehoboth Beach, Delaware through a mutual friend. Few words were spoken to each other the day of our introduction, though there was a palpable attraction. We were both involved with other women. Lori had been living with someone for three years and they already owned a house together. I was having an affair that I hoped would become permanent, but my girlfriend was not yet divorced from her husband. I know; it was complicated.

And then...Ten years later, it was a flawless September afternoon in Annapolis, Maryland, and I was walking toward Lori along the stone path that overlooks the South River at Quiet Waters Park. The gazebo that stands atop a steep hill, where I was about to become a wife, was flanked with billowing, white lilies standing on porcelain pedestals, and the seats were padded with puffy, white satin pillows.

The sun glistened off of the water as I watched Lori walk toward me, smiling and glancing toward the gazebo that held our family members and friends who would soon witness the sharing of our wedding vows. We converged at the peak of the circular approach, shifted our bouquets of calla lilies and roses to one hand, and joined our other hands to walk the last few steps we would ever take as single women.

When I looked into Lori's exquisite green eyes, the color that symbolizes freshness and vitality of life, I saw our lives spread out before us and could hardly contain my excitement for what was yet to come for us. The intimate crowd of ten included our immediate families, of which all did not outwardly endorse a same-sex marriage. But at least they were there, especially our mothers.

Christina Perri was singing "A Thousand Years" from the Bose music system. And as I heard the line, "I have died every day waiting for you," I held back the tears that would cause my chin to quiver and would have ruined the makeup that cost $150 to have professionally applied, false eyelashes and the whole deal. There were so many decades that I felt like I died waiting for my real life to begin, hiding my sexuality to please the people I loved the most.

And there I was, marrying the woman of my dreams in front of our families.

We were both wearing white dresses, each expressing our different tastes. Mine was a simple Ralph Lauren sheath that was clingy and off one shoulder. My bride chose a dress with a more intricate lace bodice and a flowing skirt that grazed her white high heels. Her blonde hair was swept up on one side and fell in curls toward her right shoulder. The dampness of the day lifted my normally straight, short hair into a pouf of waves, in a good way. My mother, wearing an elegant, navy-blue dress with silver trim and a matching blue and silver jacket, was in the front row, with an expression that was both loving and slightly wary.

A gay, married, female Episcopal priest married us. Her white robe had great fullness in the body and sleeves and flowed to the ground. When she ended the ceremony by saying "You may kiss your wife," we kissed, and knew it was the first time our families had ever witnessed the depth of our affection. They may have known we were in love, but we were sure they never allowed themselves to picture physical love between two women beyond us bumping up against each other while cooking in the kitchen. However formal our attire and the ceremony, at our core, we felt wildly free, finally unleashed.

Looking back at a long life, I see that hiding my true feelings might have been the worst decision I ever made. Being gay for all those decades meant leading a very complicated, often stressful life. From that first knowing, if I had told my mother that I liked girls, it would have seemed very innocent. She might have thought, "Oh, this will change." But at age eight, how could I tell her that I already had a crush on my music teacher, Miss Bajcura, and dreamed that someday she would be my wife? After that early crush I never, with any sincerity, envisioned a romantic relationship with a man. And so my double life began, morphing into even a triple life as the years went on.

I often reflect on how different my path would have been had I grown up in these times of gay pride and a burgeoning LGBTQ community. Kids now come out to their parents as early as elementary school, but for me, I ended up going into sexual hiding, acting out my life as if it were a performance worthy of an Academy Award.

I hung out with the girly girls, and we all talked about which boys we liked, who we thought was cute, and who we wished would ask us out. Mine was all fake talk, but that is what I had to do in order to fit in. For a long time, I thought I was the only gay person in the world. This, because I was hiding my heart.

I strung along any boys who liked me, and I pretended to be a girlfriend. I remember kissing Johnny in his swimming pool in the summer of 1962. It was enjoyable but only because he was two years older, many girls liked him, and he picked me! I did not respond to his kiss, but it was nice to know that he chose me, a sixth grader, over many other girls he could have been chasing after. I hid my crushes on Karen, Patty, Susan, and a few female teachers until the spring of my junior year in high school when "I kissed a girl and I liked it." I could have written that Katy Perry song.

That kiss turned into my first real love affair that lasted until the following summer when I left for college. Madelina–her nickname was Maddie–was one year younger and a few inches shorter than me. She was funny and Italian and had curly, auburn hair that she hated so much that she slept with her bangs taped to her forehead so they would lay flat the next day.

When pretty and feisty Maddie walked into a room, wearing her Ladybug crewneck sweater, round-collared blouse, short red skirt with matching tights, and Bass Weejun loafers, both the girls and the guys noticed. She had a wide, toothy smile and brown eyes that sparkled and made her magnetic. Her perfect posture and sexy stride revealed the confidence that oozed from her without arrogance or conceit. Her inner contentment surfaced as a power and freedom that permitted her to speak her mind without seeming aggressive.

Maddie and I met at Kaufmann's Department Store in Monroeville, where we worked during high school summers. We each had a boyfriend who visited us during work hours and our high school girlfriends came to the store and took advantage of our employee discounts. Maddie looked at me differently than I had been looked at before, and we held our gazes just a second or two longer than a normal glance during conversation. We worked in the Juniors department of the store, where we played a jukebox of Creedence Clearwater Revival hits and all the Motown one could hope for. We had a great time talking and selling to teenage girls and keeping the department attractive and in order.

While all of Maddie's qualities were attractive to me, what I liked most of all was that she liked me, openly. She gave me her attention when others were clamoring for it. Her physical endowment made the boys want her and the girls envy her, but that was not what drew me to Maddie. I knew there was something different about how we were drawn to each other, something intuitive. When she leaned in and kissed me in the stockroom, it was clear that we both liked girls, and not just as friends.

Maddie and I sneaked handholding and a few stolen kisses, and believed our relationship was totally hidden, safe and secret. Since she attended a different high school, we did not see each other every day, but the distance made it easier to keep our secret. We started meeting on our days off and would just drive around for hours. My mother thought I was with my high school friends and never questioned me or checked the mileage on the car. I was not ready to be honest about the new friend I made at work. My mother would have been suspicious, since she knew how attached I was to my tight-knit group of six best friends. I believed my mother would not understand how I got so close so fast and spent so much time with someone new and away from my peeps. Mum was always able to read my face and body language. She knew when I was nervous and was not telling the truth. So, I hid Maddie for as long as I could.

Sometimes, Maddie and I met at Blue Spruce, a swimming pool located between her house in Penn Hills and mine in Level Green. She and I lay beside each other, covered our heads with one towel and kissed underneath while sunbathing. At the same time, my friends were swimming at Blue Dell pool, located about ten miles away, so I never told them I was going to Blue Spruce and never invited them to join me. Maddie and I wore our Villager bathing suits, and she was the only girl I knew who needed a larger size on the top than she did on the bottom.

Eventually, I introduced my family to my new work friend but only after sufficient time had passed and we knew each other well enough to feign a straight friendship. She and I spent nights at each other's houses, and sometimes she even joined me on Friday night sleepovers with my hometown girlfriends. The relationship moved from kissing and handholding to full-on lovers. Then, one morning, the worst person it could have been outed to discovered our secret. Maddie had slept over, both of us in my double bed, and my mother walked into a scene of two girls hugging. Before my mother could sound an alarm, I quickly told her that my girlfriend was crying about her boyfriend. What I did not add to this false explanation was that the tears were of confusion, because she loved us both. I was horrified. My mother had interrupted a night of spooning that ended in a snuggly, romantic wakening, and Mum's expression revealed that she did not believe my feeble explanation.

While my high school boyfriends were just props, I came to know, painfully, that Maddie's were real. Even though one of my frequent dates was Chris, the popular starting quarterback, the poor guy was just a placeholder and a means to attend the events of Homecoming, the Christmas dance, and the Prom. Maddie and I had plans to move from our hometowns, far from my graduating class of 139, attend the same college, and be together forever. So much for youthful dreams.

Maddie's boyfriend hated me, and when he picked Maddie up from work and saw me, he would stick up his middle finger and glare. He approached me once and told me he did not like how close I was to his girlfriend. I thought, *Your girlfriend? She is my girlfriend!* I had no words for him and refused to engage. Soon after that parking lot encounter, he gave Maddie an ultimatum: choose him or me. She was about to begin her senior year of high school and she chose him, a man to whom she is still married.

My heart was broken, and I thought I would never get beyond that unrelenting ache and sense of abandonment. If I had spoken those six words, maybe we would have lasted longer and she would have chosen me. Again, who knows. The year was 1968, and though free love and the sexual revolution was a prevalent youth movement, gay love was still largely closeted. I will never know if she left me because of societal expectations, her Catholic patriarchal parents, or if she believed it was not okay to be gay. What was clear, though, was that Maddie made the safe choice.

I had never felt such rejection as I did when she told me she preferred a man to me. I knew our love had been authentic, but she seemed to dismiss it all matter-of-factly. A girl's best friend, who happens also to be her lover, is her lifeline. When I lost that line, I was set adrift. That brush-off was almost debilitating.

My sadness was so apparent that my new friends at college were concerned about me. I would stand in front of the jukebox at the student union and listen to one sad Smokey Robinson song after another. "Tracks of My Tears" and "Being With You" played over and over. Yet I could not share the root of my grief with my straight group of friends. I would instead pretend to be interested in their silly conversations about frat boys and sorority rush over Coke and French fries. Remembering the silent agony of that breakup, it now seems very melodramatic. But I was only seventeen years old and believed my love life was over.

Sadness, for me, needs to be shared in order to get through the grieving. I was not able to do that, so I was not able to be myself. The lonely feeling came from not being known. What made it worse is that Maddie did end up attending the same college, and I would see her from afar and dart the other way. The hurt was still so raw. I will never know if she agrees but I consider her my first love and I imagine she holds the same secret deep inside, something her husband will never know.

However deep was the pain, I did realize something important about myself during this first love relationship, and that was that I was attracted to lipstick-lesbians, not girls who looked like boys. The butch female athletes in sweat clothes who hung out on the steps of the Athletic Fieldhouse were definitely not my type. So, that is when the sexual hiding and my rendition of a straight life began.

After graduation and the weddings that followed, I faded away from some of my best friends, those same friends who supported me while I was listening to Motown and moping around the student union. Telling them the truth about myself was more than I could bear, and it meant taking a chance on losing them anyway. I needed that separation to be my choice, so I did not give them an opportunity to reject me. I did not trust those who I loved and those who I knew loved me. So, I packed my red MG and, with Western Pennsylvania in my rearview mirror, I fled for the big city of Washington, D.C., a gay-friendly town, and thus began my triple life…

chapter two

DON'T LOOK FOR LOVE IN ALL THE WRONG PLACES

WHAT IN THE WORLD was I thinking? I must have expected the lesbians of Washington, D.C. to get a message that I was in town and to crawl out of the woodwork to help me come out and acclimate into a new life. That is not exactly how it happened. Far from it.

After spending my first two years in Washington with straight roommates and many visits from college friends and family, I realized I was continuing to live the same double life I had been living in Level Green, Pennsylvania. On the sly, I made phone calls to the local colleges, asking if they had any gay organizations or could give me information about gay bars or restaurants. They would only tell me about their own clubs but nothing about gay businesses or meeting places. I did not have a cell phone, so I had to hide or be cryptic with my conversations. I had this crazy fear that each call had a direct line to the Prince George's County Public Schools where I worked, or that the person on the other end could identify me and would ruin me. So, I really was not free at all.

Keep in mind, that was the early 1970s and, despite the euphoria of the hippies unleashing of the sexual revolution, gays were still largely closeted in a strong homophobic culture. Being openly gay meant losing jobs or being bullied, or even beaten–or worse. Despite the theme of liberation, the seventies witnessed harrowing acts of violence, from the serial killer known as the Trash Bag Murderer, who preyed on young gay men in California, to the acts of arson that attacked gay churches throughout the country. Jim Downs, the author of *Stand By Me: The Forgotten History of Gay Liberation*, stated that "Some gays fought for equality and demanded political and legal recognition but most were invested in creating a culture and community of their own." Though some states were repealing their sodomy laws, it was still illegal in many states, as were same-sex relationships.

Then I overheard the conversation that changed my life. One of my straight roommates was talking to a friend of hers about a girl band that played at a women's bar in Washington. The friend was sharing how good the band was and how much fun she and her straight guy and girlfriends had at this lesbian bar. I could not believe my ears. *"Did she really say lesbian bar?"* I did my best to appear nonchalant when I tripped over the couch and knocked over a chair getting to the conversation. I needed more information and I wanted it fast. Again, acting cool, I asked the name and location of the bar. That was it.

It was a crisp October day in 1973 when I learned about Phase One, a women's bar on Eighth Street in Southeast Washington, D.C. With that little bit of information, I knew where to go to find some gay women, and I finally stepped into the gay world of Washington, D.C., a world of freedom, fulfilling my mother's greatest fear.

The timing was perfect as our landlord, who had been serving in the military, gave notice that he was returning to the area and we needed to vacate his house. I moved in with a friend of a colleague on Capitol Hill. It was a glamorous three-bedroom apartment with high ceilings, brass and crystal chandeliers, a butler's pantry, and a dumbwaiter to nowhere, which we used to store roach traps–quite glamorous. The foyer had beautiful black and white tile floors and a wide stairway with large and ornate dark wood banisters. Visitors were required to ring in, and the residents had to go down to the door to receive guests. This small building that held seven apartments and a laundry room, quite a luxury, was going to be the perfect, cool place to entertain my new set of gay friends.

I was free of roommates who knew me from college, and I was living two blocks from Phase One. I called the bar and learned that it opened at seven p.m. and showed up promptly at seven-fifteen, which I believed would be fashionably late. It was a weeknight, so I thought the crowd would be early, flowing in after work for happy hour. Well, it turns out I arrived at an empty bar, and I must have seemed like a friendless nerd when I sat at the bar, alone, and ordered a glass of red wine. I can still remember that it was Gallo Hearty Burgundy poured from a huge jug. I had not yet learned the rules of sophisticated wine snobs–not to drink anything that comes in a bottle bigger than my head.

The Phase One, a lesbian bar that operated since 1970, sadly closed its doors in 2017. When I first entered that little part of gay history, it was a dive-ish bar with no windows and a brown, painted facade that screamed, "You better know what you are doing if you enter this place." The bar was located on the left side of the room, behind was a mirrored wall, making it easy to check out passersby. The room was dark and a bit grungy and it smelled like stale beer and cigarettes. I did not care. I had found heaven.

As the bar filled with all sorts of women, some butchy, others "lipstick lesbians" like me, and even a few straight, I soon realized that I was overdressed, and I felt awkward, too nervous to start a conversation. I was wearing my school clothes, a tailored suit. The crowd that filtered in later wore jeans, graphic tee shirts, sweater vests, and all sorts of other casual attire.

I left right after I finished that first glass of wine, though I was back a few days later, properly underdressed, and eager to begin phase two of my awakening to the gay bar scene. Soon after, I met some women who invited me to meet them other evenings to play pool. Playing billiards has always been a great icebreaker for me. In a short period of time, I was easily making friends and getting asked out. Love and sex came again, this time with a newborn freedom against the elegant backdrop of my newfound home.

First, there was Annie, who taught me that "your hair is fifty percent of your looks." Thank goodness I had good hair. Her hair was short, soft, and curly, and her stylist was an Asian man at the local barber shop. Annie's instructions to him were "cut my hair one inch, no more." I was shocked, thinking that was so manly. Annie was kind and a great dancer, but we had nothing else in common, aside from a sexual attraction. To this day, I do not understand why I became so involved with her. All I can think is that it was the beginning of a period in my life when I could freely explore my God-given sexuality.

After a short time of living together, my roommate moved out to return to her job with AmeriCorps VISTA. I was thrilled to have the apartment to myself, but I couldn't afford the rent alone. Annie, a strawberry blonde smoker, and I only dated a few months before she moved in, and even transported her wall-to-wall blue shag carpet from her apartment in Arlington. I liked Annie, did not love her, and hated the carpet. Annie was always kind and happy to see me at the end of a workday. She was proud of being with a teacher and especially a person with a master's degree.

Annie introduced me to the stretches of beaches on the Maryland and Delaware shores where we spent some weekends with friends. We also joined a dining club, enjoyed getting to know the many restaurants in Washington D.C. and the surrounding area, and spent time dancing at Club Madame or Phase One, both in Southeast Washington. It was not very long before I realized, and was hurt by, some treatment I was tolerating.

When I went out of town to visit my family, Annie sometimes entertained her ex-girlfriend–in my bed–because, as she put it "She was lonely." Annie insisted that they snuggled and spooned but "nothing happened." Nothing happened? Snuggling and spooning happened and that was not okay with me. I stupidly stayed with the relationship, perhaps out of my own loneliness and need for a partnership. I had self-sabotaging thoughts that her mistreatment of me was my punishment for being gay and hiding it from my parents. I was not yet convinced that I deserved better. That was the first of many times I pretended, or hoped, to be in love.

Annie's ex-girlfriend was always in the picture and, after many months of this, I realized that was not going to change. Our routine grew dull very quickly, and even though I was not sure what I wanted; it was not that. Annie and I had been together one year when I began to break away. I was not direct and honest with her but slowly started to spend time with new friends. I remember driving away from the apartment to spend part of a weekend with a colleague from the elementary school where we both worked. Annie stood at the front window that overlooked Pennsylvania Avenue and watched as I drove away. I did not want to go, but I did not want to stay. It felt the same as when I visited my parents and then drove away. As I ventured out alone repeatedly, the break-up became clear. Annie got to keep the perfect apartment. Well, not perfect-perfect–there were roaches.

That teacher friend turned out to be a lover. Laura had attitude. She strutted into every room as if she owned the place and spoke with such confidence that she almost came off as being a know-it-all. She was tall, handsome, and a skilled athlete in tennis, golf, and softball. Friends teased Laura about her Prince Valiant hairstyle, which was a chin-length pageboy with long bangs that she curled toward her forehead. Her energy and sense of humor made her great company, platonic at the time, but I was put off by her bravado and arrogance, suspecting it could be a cover for insecurity.

Laura stayed in the closet to her family and work colleagues, just as I did. She pretended to be straight with everyone in the world except one woman, Carrie, from her hometown. That girl had moved to Maryland from New York to be with Laura. They were each other's first gay lovers, though they were masterful at cover-ups, with Laura speaking often of her ex-boyfriend and Carrie bringing up her New York man as if they were maintaining a long-distance relationship.

When Laura and I kissed for the first time, she and Carrie maintained that they were only friends. When I visited, I also spent time with Carrie, who made me laugh, was easy to talk to, and had no hidden agenda. Laura was so anal and possessive that soon I felt trapped, but I thought I was in too deep to back away. I knew she would make life miserable if I did not move forward with a relationship with her. The truth was, I saw through the facade of the straight roommates and already had a crush on Carrie. She reciprocated the feelings, but they could not be acknowledged.

It was a confusing time, but I walked away from my wonderful Capitol Hill apartment and moved in with Laura anyway. Changes happened quickly, and in retrospect, seemed uncaring and even unkind. Laura wanted Carrie out and me in. In the blink of an eye, Carrie moved back to New York. None of us was happy. We did not understand our own desires, needs, who we wanted to be or to be with. Immature and selfish decisions were being made all around.

I later learned that Laura also had a "friend" who lived in Chicago whom she visited once each year. That girl, Tina, came to Maryland once a year and somehow Laura made sure it was a weekend when I was going to Pittsburgh to visit my family. Again, wanting to make a partnership work, I wanted to believe that her intentions were good, when in truth, Laura did not want me to know that she and Tina were more than friends too. Laura convinced Tina that I was merely a roommate, just as she had convinced me about Carrie. It was all totally screwed up, but there is even more.

Several years later, Tina moved to Northern Virginia, had a girlfriend, and she and I had a little fling. We were all pretty much a mess. I had no idea what a train wreck my social life and love life were, but it surely is true that hindsight is twenty-twenty. I will never understand how I kept my professional life so orderly and well-planned, moving up the ladder to administrative positions, while my romantic life was so chaotic.

The house I moved into with Laura was owned by her ex-boyfriend, who visited too often and still wanted alone time with her. I guess I had not learned a lesson from the situation with Annie and her ex. The shit I put up with! The ex-boyfriend coming over and going behind closed doors with my lesbian lover and faking we were just friends to him was miserable. Working at the same school meant that I saw Laura in the faculty room every day and pretended that I only knew her slightly.

Laura had a routine that she expected me to adapt and made it glaringly apparent how different we were. In between classes, she graded all her papers and wrote her lesson plans so that by the time she went home, all her schoolwork was finished. She changed into her jock clothes and started the grill. Laura made herself a few rums and cokes, grilled bacon cheeseburgers, and began her evening of television shows. "Little House on the Prairie" was her absolute favorite. This, when I had schoolwork to complete and preferred relaxing by reading Colleen McCullough's *The Thorn Birds.* Though in a relationship, I felt as if I were alone.

Laura and I met Sherry at a Sunday brunch billiards tournament. Sherry was eccentric, energetic, full of humor, and very pretty. I was immediately drawn in. We socialized with Sherry often, visiting each other's homes. I was starting to get to know Sherry better and wished I could spend more time with her and less with Laura. Within a few months, Laura turned out to be bossy and mean and often drunk, having consumed too many Cuba Libres. Plus, the sex was awful and one-sided—her side. She became another one-year flash in the pan.

We were all bouncing from girlfriend to girlfriend as we moved through our twenties and thirties. Reflecting on those times, I had experienced too much heartbreak and too many breakups for that young age. My college friends were married and starting to have babies while every lesbian I knew had a list of at least four girlfriends and a few flings under their belts before reaching their late twenties. That is nothing to be proud of and I am not.

I am telling you about a few of the short-lived players in my life because I want you to understand that each of them taught me lessons about myself. Through the experience with Annie, I learned that I could walk out the door and not think too much about the broken heart I left behind. That was a terrible thing to learn, but another lesson was to never repeat that behavior. From Laura, I learned to stand up for myself. When I was being treated poorly, I needed to muster my strength and pride, understand my worth, and leave. Hiding my truth from my family made me cling to women whom I did not know well and did not love. The choices I thought I had were to stay with women who were most likely not right for me, or to be alone.

As a result, I went through that 'throw-away' period when I did not treat girlfriends fairly. That seems strange to me now because at the time, finally free to be my true self, I was so happy to be with gay people. I would think that I would have been more thoughtful and kinder. I know now that I was not. Experiencing that "throw-away" philosophy from the receiving end with Maddie, who broke my heart in high school, might have implanted the indifference in my heart. I would come to experience being thrown away at least two more times, but I justify those because the girls who did the throwing were straight.

When I walked out on Laura and moved in with Sherry, I was only twenty-seven and Sherry was thirty-two. That is when the fun began. We worked hard at our schools, and we partied hard too. I always had a second job either bartending, waitressing, or tutoring while Sherry spent most of her spare time at galleries, museums, or at her easel. I became a runner and started learning about fitness and nutrition, which I still practice. Sherry and I took photography and painting classes at The Torpedo Factory in Old Town Alexandria, where we lived. We traveled to visit friends and our siblings, who were scattered around the country, and we loved our two cocker spaniels, Becket and Pepper.

Sherry was, and still is, a very talented painter. She was full of fascinating and original ideas about art and art history. I so admired her devotion to perfecting her craft and learning about the painters who influenced her. When she visited galleries and museums, she was studying the works of great artists from Henri Matisse to Andy Warhol. Her eccentricities were more prominent when she was drinking, which she did a lot, preferring vodka. Walking drunk through the alleys of London was an attractive dream of Sherry's. She also thought it was enviable when someone was regarded as an "old salt," a sailor who told stories that may be truthful, half-truths, or falsehoods. Maybe that is why, later in life, she bought a small fishing boat and spent hours alone on that boat, taking photographs, and gathering material for still-life paintings.

Sherry was another lesbian who hid her truth from her parents. They lived several hours away, in North Carolina, rarely visited, and, like my mother and me, Sherry and her mother had shared some uncomfortable conversations, dancing around her sexuality. They thought of me as their daughter's best friend. Sherry was a genuine social animal and enjoyed her students, colleagues, bartenders, and strangers she met along the way in galleries or clubs. Being interested in topics ranging from the deep and philosophical to the quirky and even pornographic, Sherry was, and remains, a terrific conversationalist who spoke the truth and always brought levity to the table.

Sherry told stories ranging from hilarious to tragic about her college days, living in New York City and parties on Fire Island. The photographs of us usually had Sherry holding a cocktail in one hand and one of her Winstons, or what she called a "fag" in the other. She grew up in the south where cigarettes were commonly called "fags" and we always thought that was entertaining. I remained enthralled with this smart, witty, and cosmopolitan woman for seven years. She was not a throwaway girlfriend.

A conversation that changed my life took place early in my relationship with Sherry. I got another chance to unveil my truth to my mother when I was twenty-nine, and she broached the "that's me" subject again. Coming out then would have been clearly sexual and scary to her. The conversation occurred when Mum was visiting at our townhouse in Alexandria, Virginia and Sherry left us alone for some mother-daughter time. Mum was not a big drinker so I thought a sweet blender drink would be fun. I tossed the rum, triple sec, ice, and strawberries in the blender, garnished with a lime wedge, served the daiquiris, and we sat perpendicular to each other, knee-to-knee in the living room.

It was like a girls night out, and we were enjoying some light conversation when halfway through her drink, I knew trouble was coming. Mum's face grew dark. Her expression quickly volleyed between assertive and almost angry to timid and afraid. I was intimidated by my sweet and gentle mother because I feared the worst. Then I got it. Abruptly and disassociated from any subject we had been discussing, she asked "Do you have normal feelings toward men?" That damn daiquiri! The question was gut-wrenching. It felt as if she asked whether I strangled a puppy or murdered her first born. Then my mind did the rapid toggling from, *Normal? What is normal anyway?* to *How dare you ask me that!* to *Oh, just tell her the truth. How bad can it be?*

For a second or two, I thought this would be my chance to come clean. I fidgeted in my seat but, before I could get one word out, she continued by saying "Because if you don't, I'll blame myself and I don't know what I'll do for the rest of my life." Thinking "I don't know what I'll do" meant she might take her own life, I replied to this person I loved more than anyone else, "Of course I do, Mum."

Once again, I chose the coward's way out and told another lie. In retrospect, I made another huge mistake. I have gone over that moment a hundred times in the last forty years. I could have said, "Mum, I love you so much and I want you to know that I do prefer women. I need you to know my truth. I will always be your daughter and I need your acceptance and your love." Instead, I chickened out, lacking the courage to speak up for myself. Those words just did not come to me back then and, even if they had, I was too afraid of the reaction I would receive.

Sherry still remembers my remorse and anger after that conversation and my unhappiness for the next few days. I was angry that my mother was so intrusive, even though I know she was coming from a place of caring, and who knows how she would have reacted if she knew the truth? I was mostly angry and disappointed in myself. I felt spineless. The impact of those few words spoken by my mother were held deep inside me with all the guilt and secrets that accumulated over the next several years.

It was a quarter of a century after the conversation with my mother over strawberry daiquiris that I met Lori. We each owned a house in Rehoboth Beach, Delaware, and were introduced during a summer Sunday brunch where many women gathered to hear the band Divas of One Love at the Iguana Grill. Perhaps it was a foreshadowing that we would become joined in one love, though neither of us are divas. She was seated at a large table with several other women, and we did not talk past our introduction to each other. I did think, *She is very pretty and those green eyes!* I was with the girlfriend who had not yet left her husband and Lori was with her girlfriend of three years.

By the following summer I was newly single, and Lori and I began running in the same social circles. And in Rehoboth, always listed as one of the most gay-friendly towns in America, there is plenty of social life–great bars and restaurants and nightly beachfront parties.

By the time fall turned to winter, Lori and I were best friends. She confided that her four-year relationship was starting to sour, and I would confide details of the women I dated. Lori always weighed in, protective and engaged, steering me away from women she deemed unworthy as the right fit. I was hoping she was trying to keep me single because she might have another plan for us. Though for several months, I was too afraid to address my attraction that went beyond best friends. I continued to go out with multiple prospects and even went on double dates with Lori and her girlfriend. All the while, my feelings were deepening.

Lori was intriguing from the start. First off, she is gorgeous–she is vivacious, curious, and well, very sexy on top of this. She was also inquisitive, which could be off-putting and alluring. We spent many hours on the telephone and at happy hours, and there were a few times when I asked her if I was being interviewed. She actually said "Yes," and continued to dig around every corner of my life, from past loves to my parents and siblings. Lori created scenarios, real or fictitious, to learn what I would do in any given situation. As our friendship deepened over the next three years, Lori became single, too. I waited for that to happen, impatiently.

During what I now consider our unconscious courtship, our hands would touch and linger then suddenly one of us would pull away. She was living with someone, so those flirtations could not turn into a romance. In fact, it took five years between meeting Lori and embracing that romantic role. My sense that we were meant-to-be came one night when we hugged goodbye, and that hug lasted just long enough for us to know that something more was happening. We had been listening to live music and dancing at a crowded local pub. After a night that had been filled with laughs and conversations that required physical closeness due to the loudness of the band, that hug seemed to come so naturally.

chapter three

LOVE, LIES, AND MY MOTHER

MY MOTHER, NELLIE, LOVED women, this I know. Some in the superficial way of many friendships, but there might have been one that was very different. Mum belonged to a women's golf group, a women's card club, and she called herself a spotty member of Eastern Star, the female version of the Masons. She was always close to my sister, Maggie, and to me, and she had close girlfriends and cousins that were very important in her life. Nellie lived with her good friend and roommate, Peg, during their nurses' training at Columbia Hospital in Pittsburgh, and Peg turned out to be a lesbian.

Toward the end of Mum and Peg's two years living in the same room in the nurses' dorm, my mother went on a blind date with the twenty-three-year-old, gangly son of circus performers. That date turned into her forever love, my father. Not only was Peg not happy for Nellie, but Peg was also very upset about this romance and even stated that she felt like my mother left her for Bob. My mother shared this a few times, but her stories seemed to just skim the surface. The way she glazed over it made me think her light approach covered something deeper.

What was that all about? It could have come from her feelings that could not be acted upon. Of course, I was too timid to dig below that surface. Nellie was already twenty-one years old when she met Bob, so did she grab the first guy that met her minimum criteria, tall, handsome, and a good dancer? Desperation might have led to that short criteria list. I do not believe my mother was desperate to find a boyfriend, but she could have been ready to create a wall between her and Peg. Nellie could always say "No, I have a boyfriend," if she were confronted by any unwanted advances. If Nellie was driven by guilt or fear, what was she afraid of? I am only projecting, or even hoping, when I say that it seems like there was something going on that made her want to have a guy hanging around. She could have been taught that homosexuality was something to be ashamed of. Whatever the reason, she put on the brakes with Peg and found my father.

Bob had family history that could have caused him to be short-tempered, even mean, but he was quite the opposite. He was pensive and kind and always looked deep into Nellie's eyes with a sincerity that she learned to adore. Bob was well-liked by her family and was a safe escape from a non-traditional lifestyle Peg might have wanted her to join.

I asked my sister what she knew about the relationship between Peg and my mother, and I expected her to vehemently disagree with my idea that something must have gone on between the two. Instead, she expressed that she knew that Peg had "come on" to my mother. My sister agreed that the two women had an obviously strong emotional tie. Maybe it was nothing but a one-sided female crush or maybe it was something more. Everyone has secrets. Whether theirs was a realized love is immaterial. What is definite is that, for some reason, Peg felt forsaken. And when my mother spoke of Peg, there was a wistfulness to her stories, and she never looked me in the eye.

After Peg finished nurses' training, she enlisted in the Navy and remained in service until she earned an honorable Navy retirement. Peg met her forever partner, Bernie, a female, while in the Navy. Peg and Bernie visited the Pittsburgh area and got together with all the girls from nurses' training and their husbands. The female couple attended picnics at our home, and they were treated exactly like the straight couples. Bernie was a talented golfer and played golf with the men.

Peg always seemed jolly and possessed a sense of humor that was a common theme among my family and all their friends. She was proud of her career, and some of the other nurses seemed a little envious of Peg's successes and her freedom. During those visits, I noticed that my mother and Peg would go to the kitchen or make drinks together, without the others, and would giggle as if they were sharing an inside joke. Of course, I could have been hoping there was something between them. Though naive in my thinking, I could blame someone other than myself for my feelings toward girls.

My mother's close circle of nurses seemed to love their husbands and definitely cherished their children. But I heard them snicker and chat about how much easier and carefree life might be if they had female companions and not the constraint of a husband. That is back when men got away with calling their wives, "the old ball and chain." What a joke! If those men only knew who the real balls and chains were—them.

Peg's Navy career was likely very challenging when it came to her sexuality. This was the 1930s, when women were defined by their marriages to men. Being gay was not accepted; those perceived to be homosexual were called fags and dykes. The creation of LGBTQ was decades away. Although there was a gay subculture in Hollywood that included Marlene Dietrich, Tallulah Bankhead, and even Greta Garbo, who called homosexual affairs "exciting secrets," it was not in the mainstream and happening in Pittsburgh. There was no community for these people. It was hardly accepted, and even illegal.

Secrecy was key in that homophobic, unenlightened age. Even people who were gay could not acknowledge it. Silence protected reputations, as well as adding its own thrill, but secrecy meant lies and my mother was just getting to know herself during those times. I never pressed my mother about this. I never thought about it until recently.

Peg possessed that military confidence that was enough to allow her to stay in touch with her straight friends and include her girlfriend. According to my mother, Peg's gayness was never mentioned, but it was clear to me that her actions spoke louder than the unspoken words. In hindsight, my actions must have done the same and, in my case, I wish the transition to spoken words had come sooner. The fact that Peg was so obvious, and so loved, gave me a short-lived hope about coming out. For a brief time, I actually considered joining the military, thinking it was a place to find other lesbians and have clandestine affairs.

I remember the conversation that took place while I was in college, again in my mother's kitchen, where most of our long, heart-to-heart talks took place. Mum spoke about Peg, blushed a little, but was brief in saying that she left for Bob and that Peg was hurt. She told me Peg felt she abandoned her. I was afraid to ask too many questions about Peg. I thought it would incriminate me that I shared her lifestyle, imagining that my head would split open and start spewing information like a Teletype machine printing out news updates. So, once again, I needed to keep my mouth shut and even feign indifference to the story.

How close were they? Maybe it was her own guilt of having feelings for a woman that made her so protective of me. Maybe my mother's friendship with Peg was the beginning of her fear of homosexuality, which I understand. It was the 1930s, after all. I doubt if my mother knew much about homosexuality, so she did not know if it was contagious or genetic and may have feared that she passed homosexual tendencies along to me. There were secrets between my mother and me since my early childhood, and there are secrets she took to the grave that I will never know. I see now that some of those secrets might have been chilling in those homophobic decades.

My mother was from a very traditional background. Though her life began by seeing the earth suck up four loved ones, Nellie saw her mother carry on and raise five children. Mum followed the rules, became a nurse, and was expected to marry and have children and be a dutiful wife. She was June Cleaver. In some ways, Mum was the template for the traditional life I now live–married, two dogs, and a van. Despite two parents who loved me and the life of stability and normalcy they provided, I took off in a different direction, one still considered abnormal by many folks.

Even in the sixties, when Nellie started to worry about her youngest child, gays were openly dishonored even though the gay rights movement was gaining momentum. I could not find my motivation to come out. Some find it very late in life, too late to share it with the most important people. All I wanted was for my parents to love me, listen to me, and accept me exactly as I was. I had a fear that being gay might make me disposable to them, especially my mother. I had witnessed my neighbor's rejection of his gay son, and I thought that could happen to me too.

I surmised that my mother disapproved of homosexuality and would try to change me. I had not heard of conversion therapy at the time, but I knew that my paternal grandmother was given shock treatments for mental illness. What if they wanted to do the same thing to me? Possibly because of those fears, I wasted many good years with my parents by choosing to stay in the closet. What I did not know was that they would live another forty years, so the number of lost years was going to be very high. So, reader, tell your people.

Who was my mother really? Was she the sad four-year-old, the youngest child of a widow, who lost her father and two brothers in one year? Was she the naïve, clarinet-playing teenager who proudly wore the beautiful homemade clothes her mother tailored for her? Could she have simply been the studious nursing student and the hard-working and focused nurse who went back to college in her forties to become a school nurse so her work hours could match the school hours of her children?

Was her truth within the church volunteer who crocheted hats and made Steeler dammit dolls for the church bazaar and the baker who made ten dozen rolls for the Methodist pork and sauerkraut dinner on Election Day? She was certainly the devoted mother who loved and nurtured each of her children so perfectly that each of us thought he or she was her favorite. And she was the ninety-six-year-old who still volunteered at Pittsburgh Children's Museum, helping the children with their crafts.

My mother was June Cleaver minus the pearls. Also unlike June, after eighteen years of motherhood, she did get a full-time job. She cooked every meal, washed every piece of clothing, and kept the house clean while assigning few chores to her children. She trained all of us well and sent us into the world knowing how to take care of ourselves, make a meal, pay our bills, and be fair, kind, and honest. As engaged as my mother was in our upbringing and as open and honest as she seemed to be, some things about her remain mysteries. She and I had that in common.

Might Mum have been a closet lesbian who loved Peg and broke her heart by taking the easy road and settling down with a man? If that is the case, she made a wonderful life for her husband and children and played the perfect mother and wife until she died at the age of ninety-eight.

I had two parents and a stable home but still had to escape the nest. Without saying the words, my mother probably always knew I was different from her friends daughters, who were marrying right out of college. Perhaps she knew it as early as when I was eight and asked her, "What is a queer?" I missed the "that's me" moment so many times. To understand why I missed those moments, you need to know more about my mother.

***

Nellie Jane Devroude Mills (1917-2015)

Nellie Jane Devroude was born on March 27, 1917. Seventeen days later, the United States entered World War I by declaring war on Germany in response to German submarines, called U-Boats, sinking United States ships. That start of World War 1 was also the same spring Suffragists marched to the White House in an effort to win women the right to vote. Other cultural uprisings included investigations of homosexual activity that resulted in students being expelled from colleges, including Harvard, where a Secret Court, made up of five administrators, investigated and expelled or severed association with eight students, and military arrests and trials at Naval Station Newport in Rhode Island that ended with the court martial of seventeen sailors charged with sodomy and "scandalous conduct."

Seven Devroude Siblings, 1919
(Joseph, Jr., Andrew, Frances, Charles, John, Anthony, Nellie)

As an infant, Nellie slept through many important moments in American history. In the world of early childhood, the toddler's memories were few and vague. Nellie did not remember when her oldest brother died of the Spanish Flu early in 1921, but with great clarity, she remembered the tragic accident she witnessed later that same year. It was a trauma that affected the little girl profoundly, and she carried it with her the remainder of her life. Nellie's father, uncle, neighbor, and oldest remaining brother were swallowed by the earth in what seemed to be an abyss in the family's backyard.

Every spring, Nellie's father, Joseph, dug a huge hole near the standing outhouse with the purpose of draining the cesspool of human waste. This made the outhouse functional for another year. At age sixteen, it was Nellie's brother Andrew's job to help his father with the arduous and disgusting task. The cavernous hole needed to measure six feet deep. After several hours of digging, their clothes drenched in sweat, the father and son had reached the desired depth and Andrew jumped down to poke an opening between the new hole and the existing cesspool. This was not a moment to take lightly. Before Andrew could lift his sharp blade to start the job, he was overcome by toxic gas fumes emanating from the old cesspool. His first breath inside the pit was a gasp instead as it contained so little oxygen and he collapsed immediately, slumping to the bottom. Within seconds, he lost consciousness and died.

Three more men were killed when they jumped in, one after the other, in an attempt to rescue him and then each other. My grandfather, Joseph, my great uncle, Eugene, and the next-door neighbor, Mr. Chilcotte, perished along with Andrew. Nellie's mother, Frances, was frantic as she raced over to the tragic scene, only to find the men she loved lifeless and heaped one on top of the other. Nellie resurrects the horrific scene she witnessed from the porch, at the age of four, with remarkable clarity, recalling her confusion as to whether her mother was screaming with laughter or with terror.

Nellie at four years old

Sliding along the railing of the back porch, one foot at a time, Nellie edged toward the yard then stood frozen in place, as she realized her mother was shrieking and crying as if she were insane. Frances heard Nellie whisper, tears running down her velvety toddler cheeks, "Daddy" when she heard her mother scream, "They are all dead!" Uncle

Eugene's and Mr. Chilcotte's wives heard the screaming and came running from the duplex they shared next door. There was no telephone to call for help, so Frances ran to the front street to beckon any assistance she could find while the other two women collapsed in the backyard, sobbing and moaning at the realization of what they had just learned. Only after a young male neighbor ran to the nearby firehouse did the firetruck, that doubled as an ambulance, come to the aid of the ladies, but it was too late to help the men.

That unthinkable accident in my mother's life seemed to recur as the black hole she feared for me. I have spoken to Holocaust survivors who are over-protective of their children, fearing they will lose them, too. Though Nellie was not a survivor of Hitler, that black hole seemed to instill a fear in her about me, the child she was closest to. It was as if she was afraid that I would fall into a black hole of what she thought of as the sordid, gay scene in Washington, D.C.–the city she called "Sin City."

I tried to tell my mother, before the days of intense political correctness, that Washington, D.C. was actually called "Chocolate City," but because of its reputation for riots and division, she believed it was a magnet for sinful people who pushed the boundaries of cultural norms in their politics and their lifestyles. This was, after all, 1973, when young people were protesting the war in Vietnam, the sexual revolution was underfoot, and the Watergate scandal was unfolding. My mother, a woman of constant positivity, was clearly quite the opposite about "Sin City."

Nellie always relied on prayer to get her over any hurdles she faced in life. She attended church every Sunday and said her prayers, sometimes aloud, each night after she turned out the light next to her side of the bed. Nellie prayed for her children and worried about our futures, our safety, and our happiness. Since I remained single the longest, my mother probably prayed for me the most. I believe many of those prayers were directed at wanting something different for me. Something unlike what she knew was true. Fortunately, my mother never knew that while she was lying in bed praying, I was out bar hopping and bartending, dating a stable of Ms. Wrongs.

Nellie did not remember many details of the funerals or the deep grief her mother and older siblings suffered. Though the flashback of that black day of death and sorrow was seared somewhere deep within, a pain came to the surface in odd and unexpected ways. Most prevalent was when she worried that I would be swallowed by a foreign sinful city and lifestyle and, of course, she was scared. That was the same year an arsonist burned the Upstairs Lounge, a gay bar in New Orleans, killing thirty-two people, and the same decade openly gay San Francisco city supervisor, Harvey Milk, was assassinated, and five teenage boys in Key West beat Tennessee Williams.

Nellie's widowed mother, who was only thirty-nine years old at the time, raised her and her remaining four siblings. The family's income had come from her father's job as a streetcar conductor, so the family was left with no income and no insurance money from the accident.

When I think of my mother's tenacity and resilience, I know she was imprinted by her own mother. After the accident, my grandmother rolled up her sleeves and utilized her skills as a seamstress and excellent cook, earning money from the neighbors in urban Pennsylvania by sewing and selling baked goods. She filled in with added income as a midwife, working with a local doctor on what was largely home births at the time.

Watching my mother at the sewing machine and creating magic in the kitchen with her own recipes allowed me to inherit skills as a chef and seamstress. Nellie was always proud of the clothes her mother made, as I was proud of the outfits Mum made for me. When I wore the cream-colored three-piece suit (like John Travolta's in Saturday Night Fever), the camel wool coat, or the slacks with the front pleats, I was always proud to tell my friends and colleagues that my mother had made them. And just like Nellie's friends, mine wanted to borrow my homemade clothes, but I was not as generous as my mother had been.

I was proud and protective of everything Nellie, even her sewing projects. My love of clothing and fashionable things started with my mother's ability to make any outfit I desired. Even when we could not afford expensive clothes, my mother could buy the fabric and the pattern that I chose, and get to work creating a dress, coat, or suit to match anything my friends could have purchased. Reflecting on my wardrobe choices, I seemed to choose the more tailored styles, but they were always feminine, and I loved, and still do, to accessorize.

My attire smashed the myth, and my mother's fear, that a lesbian might choose men's clothing. That was never true for me, and over the past sixty plus years, I have only known a handful of gay women who dressed in a masculine way. Even they were more athletic than manly. I also have that athletic side, but you will never see me resembling anything macho.

I heard many stories about my mother and my grandmother working together on sewing projects, especially Mum's wedding dress. Nellie wanted something tailored that she could wear for other occasions. She and my grandmother found a beautiful, dark purple wool fabric that had a tapestry-like texture. The dress was elegant with a scalloped neckline and a matching jacket. The tales of my parents' courtship made me wistful that I would not have this type of storybook, culturally accepted romance and marriage because, for one thing, it was not what I wanted, but also because there were no same-sex rights for gays.

During the Thanksgiving holiday in 1939, my father asked my grandmother for her blessing before he asked for my mother's hand in marriage. Nellie was delighted with the ring Bob had chosen and her eyes welled with tears when she saw it the first time. The ring was a two-tone European Cut, illusion-set engagement ring. It had an 18-carat yellow gold band and a white gold, filigree design that held the tiniest speck of a diamond on top. I envied that ring, thinking I would never wear one. My father replaced that original ring and wedding band with a more modern diamond ring and band on their twenty-fifth anniversary. Little could I ever imagine that would be me in fifty years, wearing a gorgeous diamond ring of my own. I keep my mother's original in my jewelry box and look at it with deep love and admiration for my parents.

Mum and Dad were married on March 20, 1940, in the Methodist Church in Turtle Creek, Pennsylvania, with a gathering of family and friends that totaled no more than thirty guests. It was obvious that Nellie loved Bob very much, and they were also best friends for the entire length of their marriage that lasted sixty-eight years.

When I think about their strong and loving relationship, I remember my mother telling me that "It's just as easy to fall in love with a rich man as a poor man." I was never quite sure if that was her way of telling me to hold out for someone who had a good income and could provide a nice life for me or if she was just hoping it would be a man. By the time I was ready to get engaged and there was a totally different scenario for me, her rich comment just made me bent on always making my own money and never depending on a man or anyone. Many times, I wondered if Mum wished she had held out for a rich man or had not ended up with a man at all.

Mum and Dad's wedding photo, 1940

Nellie had been a Methodist her entire life and remained faithful to that religion. She was motivated by her belief in God and her faith in Jesus. She spoke to Jesus every night in her prayers and after June 17, 2008, she spoke to my father too.

The United Methodist Church's 2016 Book of Discipline Statements says, "The practice of homosexuality is incompatible with Christian teaching." However, it also states that the UMC commitment is "not to reject or condemn lesbian and gay members and friends." My poor mother must have been very confused. She could hardly bear that the daughter she loved so much would one day get married to a woman. If only Nellie knew that someday she would be sitting in the front row of her daughter's wedding, witnessing two women becoming each other's wives. At least she could hold onto the Methodist tenet, "Ceremonies that celebrate homosexual unions shall not be conducted in our churches." We got hitched in a lush park on the Chesapeake Bay.

chapter four

GIRLS WILL BE GIRLS

BEYOND MY MOTHER'S CURT answer, when I was very young, to my question, "What is a queer?", there was other evidence of my mother's sensitivity to girls liking girls. When I was only seven years old, my friend, Treena, and I were playing in one of the bedrooms at her house. We had made a tent out of sheets and blankets on the bottom half of the bunkbeds. While playing with our dolls and teddy bears on our pretend camping trip, as I had often done at home and at other friends ' houses, Treena's mother threw open the bedroom door, stomped in with my mother at her side, and bellowed, "What are you girls doing under there?"

Now my answer would be, "What the hell do you think we're doing? We're playing camping trip with our dolls." I was scared and startled and hurt by the tone, the volume, and the accusation that I did not understand. Even my mother's expression made me feel like we were doing something bad or "dirty" under those sheets. Yet, at that very young age, I had no idea what it could be.

During the car ride home, when I asked why she was mad at me, I did not get a clear and fair answer from my mother. This vague accusation I was too young to comprehend still made me feel like we had been doing something horribly wrong. This, when I knew we were innocent girls at play. Though this happened more than six decades ago, I can still hear the sharpness in her voice and can still feel the confusion and guilt that came after.

I had a lot of friends in my neighborhood, and I spent my time with both the boys and the girls. I played with Candy, Judy, and Janet, doing the things little girls do. We played house with our dolls, romped in the snow, and made fudge. But I also played with the boys. I rode my bike everywhere with my best friend, Chris, while our dogs, Peppy and Pal, ran alongside. We played football and baseball with Danny and Paul, and I was the only girl the boys let play on their pick-up football team. I was brave and reckless as I ran through the woods and stomped through the creeks with the boys.

I was comfortable with both the girls and the boys, but the boys always had more fun, and I enjoyed being the only girl who joined them. In that way, I was different from the other girls, but I never thought about any other contrast. I was more athletic and stronger and braver than the other girls, maybe a tomboy, but I was not ostracized from the girls or bullied by either gender.

My sister hated that I ran around with the boys and she would lean out the front door and yell, "Jan, Mum wants you," while I was playing football across the street from our house. I would run home to check in with my mother, who denied having requested my presence. I asked my mother to "make her stop," so she calmly instructed Marge to stop calling me inside. My sister was four years older and more interested in hair and makeup, so I might have been too much of a tomboy for her, and for my mother too, but my mother never pushed me to play more with girls.

No matter who I played with or what I did, the bonds between my sister and me and my brother and me were always strong. That closeness imitated my mother's intimacy with each of her siblings. Their closeness was likely strengthened because they lost their father and two brothers when the five remaining children were ages four to fourteen. My mother had a brother who was serious and protective, one who was gentle and kind, and one who needed protection from himself and his alcohol. As they aged, Mum's sister, the oldest child, who always looked out for her little sister, and all her brothers grew to rely most on their little sister, Nellie.

Relatives described Nellie, exactly like her mother, as being "the best of human beings." She was everybody's cheerleader and loved her children almost more than she could bear. Everyone was welcome in our home. We shared what we had, even when it wasn't much. When my mother could not give in a monetary way, she gave her time, her heart, and her hard work. Though my mother was married to a man and very religious, she was who I wanted to be. At the heart of her was the heart of me, a provider who just wants to be truthful, loved, and understood. When I was sad, confused, and scared of who I was, her feelings and fears mirrored mine. It took thirty years too long to realize how alike we really were.

What would be a surprise to my mother's friends and our relatives is that she executed some crafty deeds in her effort to handle my gayness. That tells me how desperate she must have been. And all I did was try to ignore it. I discovered one of her undercover accomplishments very late in my mother's life. I chose to let it go rather than address it and I will never completely understand how my kind and compassionate mother was able to perform those few surprising and hurtful acts.

One occurred while she was visiting my apartment on Capitol Hill in Washington, D.C. My mother read a journal I kept when I was living with Annie, my girlfriend of six months. It was only a social record and calendar but reading that we went to Club Madame at least four nights each week must have been curious and disturbing to my mother. I am sure she must have thought it was a gay bar, but if she knew about the Sunday drag shows and the crazy after-hours parties in the apartment upstairs from the bar, she would have worried even more.

I never dreamed she would have the nerve to read a private journal, let alone ask me about it while she was staying at my home, but she did. My mother just came right out with, "What is Madame's?" I replied, "What do you mean? Where did you hear that?" Looking me straight in the eye, Mum told me, "I read it in that book on the shelf." She pointed to the few cookbooks and the journal leaning against the wall of the butler's pantry between the kitchen and the dining room. If something is sitting on a shelf in your house, does that make it fair game for anyone to peruse? I should have hidden the journal, or I should have just told her the truth. Again, a missed opportunity to come clean, yet out came another cover-up.

Without hesitation, I told her that Madame's was a palm reader in Arlington. It was a little frightening how quickly that lie blurted from my mouth. Of course, she knew I was lying, and she told me it was in my journal way too often to be a palm reader, but I did not turn the table back to her and tell her she should not have been reading my private journal anyway. I just shrugged and stayed with my story.

That was the first time I ever thought my mother was capable of sneaking behind my back to gather information she suspected about her daughter. My parents never determined rules of privacy with their children. We seemed to always understand that a closed door meant you had to knock before entering and that it was inappropriate to go through someone else's drawers or closets. We respected each other's property and I always asked if I could borrow something that did not belong to me.

I did read my sister's diary once but there was nothing juicy, just some preteen talk about crushes on boys. The juicy stuff would have been found in a diary of mine, had I kept one, in the eleventh and twelfth grades. Stories about what was happening between my girlfriend and me at group sleepovers when our friends fell asleep or when we went parking down deserted roads in my parents' car would have raised the hairs of the entire community, and I cannot even imagine what shame or punishment would have resulted had we been caught. As frightened as we were of being discovered, Maddie and I took some dangerous chances.

When I moved away from my parents' house, I took most of my possessions with me. I took what I needed and what I wanted at the time, but thankfully, my mother left my bedroom untouched, or that is what I believed. It took until I bought a house in 1981, eight years after leaving Level Green, Pennsylvania, that I felt real permanence and removed all my things from Sunset Drive. My mother was happy to help me go through the closets that contained prom gowns and bridesmaid's dresses.

As I combed through my remaining possessions, I started to fear that my mother might have gone snooping when I was not there or that she would find something during our cleanup. She might have uncovered my secret life before I was ready to air my truth. At that point, I was careful to take my yearbooks from high school and college. There were messages in those yearbooks that were private, and I was fearful of being discovered. That is part of leading a secret life. You are always on guard. I remember getting a twinge in my chest when I realized what my mother could have read.

Other than containing incriminating messages, I am not sure why those yearbooks were so important, but I still keep them today. My mother asked me about the full-page inscription my high school girlfriend, Maddie, wrote in my yearbook. She was curious about one line that read, "your emotions aren't worth the trouble they cause," and asked me what that meant. With my typical avoidance, I shrugged and told her I had no idea what that meant. "Who knows what she was talking about" was my response, this about a girl with whom I had some of my first kisses.

Even thirteen years after my high school graduation, I knew exactly what it meant, because I was a lesbian in love with that girlfriend and we were both pretending to have boyfriends. Sometimes her pretense with the boyfriend seemed too real and was deeply upsetting to me. In a stack of old photos, there was a picture of me with my date at the senior prom. Just looking at my face brought back that ache I carried because I wanted to be with Maddie, not David.

The yearbook came along with me to Maryland and stayed in a box with photos and other memorabilia from high school and college. I probably looked through that box once every ten years just to get rid of the things that were once meaningful but had become meaningless over time. The last time I glanced through my yearbook was after Lori and I moved into our Annapolis house in 2010.

I was sitting on the floor of the walk-in closet in one of our guest rooms. I use that closet for my clothing overflow, for personal items that do not fit into my larger walk-in, and for keepsakes that I am not ready to trash. The box that contained my school memories was fun to go through, so I was ready to enjoy the trip down memory lane. It had been customary to have each of your classmates sign your yearbook before graduation, so I looked forward to reading some of the amusing tidbits written by those teenagers I once knew.

I opened my 1968 high school yearbook with gleeful anticipation of seeing what had been written more than forty years prior. The yearbook was blank. I was stunned and could not speak for a few minutes. I rechecked the date of the yearbook and looked through the box in case I had two copies of the same year. There was no duplicate and that was definitely the yearbook from the year of my high school graduation.

Every signature, drawing, and message was gone. My stomach ached, I got tingles down my arms, and my earlobes got hot. That is my standard visceral reaction to fear, like when I just miss being in a car accident. I could not move for a few minutes. I knew instantly that my mother had taken my yearbook, bought another one, and traded it for this blank. I still believe that her fear of my lesbianism forced her to get rid of any physical evidence of its existence. A full-page note written by Maddie must have demonstrated a close relationship that my mother needed to erase. And so, she did.

My mother could try to erase the possibility of a gay daughter from her mind, though that gay daughter was growing stronger in her identity and courage with every passing day. The in-charge attitude from my professional life was finally pouring into my personal and social situations. I did have control of my life and I was convinced that I could come out at any time to anyone. But it remained my choice to keep life simpler by remaining private.

Mum was still living when I discovered the switch, and I was so angry and disappointed that I was not sure how to handle it. After all, at that point, she was at least ninety years old. Was it really worth a confrontation? No. But, I must admit, it almost made me feel good that she might do something so sneaky. In a weird way, it lessened my guilt for all my years of lies and deception, so I never asked if she stole the book.

Every day of my life, I knew that my mother would run to my rescue if I needed her, and I always felt grateful that God made her my mother. The few clashes and covert acts paled in juxtaposition to all the wonderful gestures of unconditional love I received from my mother. Mum spent years searching for honesty, but I did not want to break her heart simply because I had access to it.

My mother answered the telephone every time I called, which is more than I can say I did for her. She greeted me at the back door every time I came to visit. She made sure I was always warm and fed. My sister and I even had a running joke when my mother would tell me to put on a jacket. It did not matter whether I was cold or not; she wanted me to be comfortable. So I started saying, "Put a coat on. Your mother's cold." We laughed every time.

Looking into my mother's hazel eyes that always carried a slight sadness, I knew that was the purest love I would ever find. I also know that I continued to disappoint as I simultaneously made her proud. It is my belief that there was only one area of disappointment and several of pride. She was careful to make sure I knew that.

Where I came from and the lessons learned from my parents framed who I am, but what I chose every day determined what I have become. J. D. Vance wrote in his memoir, *Hillbilly Elegy.* "My family is not perfect, but they made me who I am and gave me chances that they never had." The author goes on to talk about his future, but most of mine is already gone. What I am, and whatever the future still has for me, is my family's shared legacy and I am grateful for it.

chapter five

MY TRIPLE LIFE

I BEGAN PLAYING TWO characters in my own life the minute I kissed my high school girlfriend. Nothing was the same after that. I continued to be the obedient daughter, the honor student, and the second-best dancer in my class, according to the yearbook votes. I drove my friends around in my parents' 1965 Chevrolet Impala Super Sport convertible, danced and sang in Command Performance, our May Day production, and was the school's top math student, in line with my SAT score. However, there was another person inside that was only allowed to surface when I was alone with my girlfriend.

I tucked that second person away when I attended college and became completely gay-inactive. I lived in a bubble of secrecy. Gradually, I learned that the hidden Jan was really the only Jan, but she was not allowed to own a solitary role in my body yet. I did not know how to set her free, but when I finally moved into a larger world where gays were marching for their rights and some were open with their families and colleagues, at least I knew I was not alone.

Many of us have double lives in some way, being one person at home and another at work, or one individual with our families and a dissimilar personality with friends. My situation was not one of just different clothes and different behaviors and conversations. The third player in my life was conceived when I became a schoolteacher. By day, I pretended to be straight as I taught my students and chatted in the faculty room with women about their male dates and husbands and children. As soon as I closed my car door in the teachers' parking lot, I became the lesbian who was only permitted to surface after work hours.

It was no longer all right with me to hide my true self who retreated in college. I remained a devoted daughter, trusted sister, and dedicated schoolteacher, but once I learned about Phase 1, the women's bar in Washington, D.C., I jumped in with both feet and did exactly what my mother feared. I fell into the black hole of gay life. The only places I knew I could find people like me were gay bars. Making new, gay friends led to the exclusion of many of my straight friends from college, who were living in the D.C. area and had talked me into moving there. I became too busy living my outed life on Friday and Saturday nights, and that was a life that did not include them. Nor was it a life I wanted them to discover–yet.

My first eight years of teaching were spent in three different elementary schools. When enrollment numbers drop, the newest teachers are usually transferred to other schools, and that was my situation for the first few years. Those moves provided opportunities to make many professional friends, and I did socialize with some in each school. School friends were never privy to my secret evening life, so occasionally, I was asked to go out on a date with a fix-up by colleagues. I always refused, claiming to work a second job with no time for dating.

By the time I requested a transfer from the elementary level to high school, I was living with Sherry in the townhouse where the infamous strawberry daiquiri was served to my mother. We had a group of girlfriends who lived across the street. Sherry and I called their home "the gay house" because there were always three to five roommates and sometimes a revolving door of different partners. They became our second family. In that house, many cocktail hours, dinner parties, and crab feasts brought friends from all around the Washington area.

The women living in the gay house were young professionals. One was an economist at the World Bank, another was a librarian at the Library of Congress, and Carrie, from the Laura days, worked at Arlington Hospital. The attractive and professional women who are also queer would have shocked my mother. Others worked solely at restaurants and bars and at least three of them had second jobs bartending or waitressing, like I did. We joined together and played on a lesbian softball team at West Potomac Park in Washington. All these activities were kept secret from my school life. I did tell my parents about playing on a softball team, but I lied and told them it was coed. Still the coward.

While there were many high points to this emancipating period of my life as I flexed and grew into my true self, there were also low points. In the fall of 1978, a rock that was thrown in the door while I was behind the bar at Phase 1 hit me. A young boy, probably between ten and twelve years old, with his buddies behind him, opened the door, yelled, "Queers!", threw the rock toward the bar, and ran away. I was always aware of the door opening and kept an eye on who entered. I saw the boy pull his arm back and I saw the rock in his hand as his elbow raised and began its forward motion toward me. I ducked to my left just before it struck my right shoulder.

A few of the women in the bar jumped to their feet and ran to pursue the young boys. When they reached the sidewalk, sound minds prevailed, and the women were satisfied with yelling obscenities. Most of the patrons stayed seated and appeared to take the attack in stride. I was just happy that the rock missed my face. I now realize how much danger was in those turbulent times. In 1980, Bob Jones III, a fundamentalist minister, visited the White House with other ministers to urge President Jimmy Carter to oppose any extension of the Civil Rights Act to homosexuals. Jones made these comments: "But it would not be a bad idea to bring the swift justice today that was brought in Israel's day against murder and rape and homosexuality. I guarantee it would solve the problem posthaste if homosexuals were stoned, if murderers were immediately killed as the Bible commands." It took Jones thirty-five years to apologize for his comments.

Sherry got a gun pulled on her while leaving The Other Side, a gay disco and restaurant in a seedy part of Southwest Washington. We also worked there, me in the dining room and Sherry on the floor of the disco. Sherry had a few cocktails under her belt and, in her cool, inebriated fashion, talked the guy out of robbing her. I remember her saying, "Just be cool. You don't want to do this." He ran away.

In those days, cops were usually in their cars close to the exits of all the gay bars, eager to catch a drunken gay person. They arrested anyone who looked tipsy and got into a car to drive. I know anyone driving under the influence should be arrested, but the Washington cops, who clung closely to the bars that blacks and gays populated, had a strong element of entrapment. It was discrimination, pure and simple, and I do not know one straight, white person who had experiences like mine.

Sunday nights were especially full of fun at the bars. The drag queens at Club Madame would use the main bar area as their sewing room on Sunday afternoons. If we were next door at the Townhouse having brunch, our frequent flyer status allowed us access to the back entrance to Club Madame that was connected to the restaurant. Sometimes, my friends and I would talk and laugh with the drags while they sewed and sequined their dresses in preparation for their show. Drag shows were happening all over town and they lasted into the wee hours of Monday morning. I saw way too many finales, but by the next morning, I had showered, fixed my hair and makeup, and began my other life as a schoolteacher on time.

Some of the guys who performed in the shows became friendly enough with me that I offered two of them tickets to the National Theatre. Sherry and I had tickets for a performance of "A Matter of Gravity," starring Katherine Hepburn, and for some crazy reason, we were not able to attend. We had planned to go with two of my school friends and when we needed to sacrifice our tickets, I never gave it a thought that I should be careful about who I seated next to the female teachers, Kathy and Joan, who did not know about my private life. I told the ladies that I gave the tickets to two men I knew from a restaurant in D.C. What they imagined beyond that was on them. The two gay guys were tall, handsome, and clean-cut, and were thrilled to receive tickets to see Hepburn. I knew they probably could not afford the tickets themselves, and what gay man would pass up a chance to see Katherine Hepburn?

The Sunday night after the performance, Sherry and I ran into the guys at Club Madame and they effused all over themselves about the show and the wonderful performance by Miss Hepburn. You would have thought they had gotten close enough to genuflect and kiss her ring. They were so happy and had such a wonderful evening. We felt like we had done the right thing to give them the seats without charge. It was a definite win-win situation with one surprise yet to come.

When I got to school the next day, Kathy and Joan also went on and on about the wonderful play and how exciting it was to see Katherine Hepburn in person. They giggled so much that I wondered what else they had to say. Finally, one of them asked how well I knew the guys who received the other two tickets. I explained that it was a passing friendship born out of frequenting a restaurant on Capitol Hill where they worked. I knew there was more to this story so I asked, "Why?"

Unbeknownst to me, Kathy and Joan had talked about who might be seated next to them and even shared that it might be an opportunity to meet possible prospects for dating. Were they ever in for a surprise! When the "gentlemen" reached the row and daintily stepped over other patrons to reach the seats beside Kathy and Joan, they were in full and formal drag that included floor-length, sequined gowns, high heels and, of course, boas. Kathy described the flurry and tittering in the audience when the men, who were at least six-foot, six-inches tall including the heels and the bouffant wigs, sashayed down the aisle and dramatically took their seats.

Fortunately, Kathy and Joan found it hilarious, but they did wonder if I knew the guys would be dressed that way and, if so, why I did not warn them. I was so far in the closet that I could not admit that I knew the men were gay. I feigned complete shock and surprise, laughed with the girls, and acted embarrassed, not that I might be connected to the gay world but that I was naive enough to have no idea these men were gay. Behind their backs, I laughed at the men and with the girls, completely denying my people. I was ashamed that I was still a coward.

My secret life continued when I worked in the catering department at the J.W. Marriott Hotel in Washington, D.C. There were many gay waiters and waitresses like me in their employ, but the Mormon-owned chain had no tolerance for homosexuality so, once again, into the closet. At least I could share stories about work and tell the truth about meeting some of the Marriott's and working a prom where Ted Koppel, the legendary broad cast journalist, was a chaperone. Telling the truth felt good because the triple life was exhausting and insulting. I also had the opportunity to work with one of the young, up-and-coming Marriott's while he trained in the catering department. He was kind, hardworking, handsome, and gay (but Daddy and Grandpa Marriott did not know that). You gotta love it!

After living with Sherry for seven years, it was apparent that her alcohol consumption was out of control, and it was time for her to spend some time in a rehabilitation facility in nearby Bethesda, Maryland. After a month there, I was included in her exit interview. At that meeting, the therapist asked if I planned on staying with Sherry after she got out of rehab. She was clarifying all the changes that would need to take place and all the support Sherry would need when she got home.

In my heart, I knew I would not stay but I could not bring myself to tell them. I knew I was not willing to change my life that had turned really fun again. I was a coward. I said, "Sure, I will be there for her." This when, during her month away, I had developed deeper friendships with women who were fun and stable. One particular person became more than just a friend. She was also a schoolteacher, beautiful, adventurous, and easy to be with after a relationship with an unstable partner with an addiction left me feeling so overwhelmed.

Seven years with Sherry crumbled irreparably in that one month. One week after she returned home, Sherry and I were having lunch at

Mr. Henry's on Pennsylvania Avenue when she asked me how long I had been sleeping with someone else. I was honest, she walked out the door, and we were finished. Just like that. By lying to Sherry, I hurt the woman who has been important in my life since 1978. For the remainder of my life, the way I treated her at that time is one of the handful of events I am most ashamed and regretful of. I thank God for our friendship, for Sherry's strength to become sober, and for her patience and forgiveness toward me. I was not there in the way she needed me then, but we are always there for each other now. For this, I will be eternally grateful.

I spent the next three years with Teresa, the woman I chose over Sherry. Whatever I was going through was harder on those around me than I realized. I was selfish and was moving through life focused on myself rather than being kind and giving to others. I was not ready for a forever relationship but I pretended to be until I did not. Then I left and expected to be forgiven.

I hurt Teresa deeply and walked away from a three-year relationship that could have lasted forever. It is more difficult to talk about that partnership than any other. I had cheated on Teresa for no good reason. She knew it and was still willing to forgive me and to give our love a second chance. I told her that I was too ashamed of what I had done, that she did not deserve that treatment, and I did not deserve her. I will never understand why I did what I did and why I did not jump at the opportunity to make it right. I let it all happen too quickly, almost repeating the behaviors from ten years prior during the Laura/Carrie debacle. Teresa and I were both heartbroken, but I never let her know how I felt.

At thirty-seven years old, I still did not know what I wanted or who I wanted to be with. I sabotaged that relationship, and my life at the time, because easy and happy was so unfamiliar to me. I owned a house that I loved, and I threw away a happy relationship two months before running to Rehoboth. I could not figure out where I belonged. The person I should have been able to create, one I would like and respect, seemed just out of reach.

That summer I took my cocker spaniel, locked up my house in Cheverly, Maryland, and headed for Rehoboth Beach. I landed a job bartending at Papa John's Beach Bar on the boardwalk. I also helped at a gay guesthouse, The Beach House, in exchange for a bedroom and a shared bathroom in the basement. The bed and breakfast was clean and tastefully decorated, just as the clientele of mostly gay men expected.

The ten-room house was usually filled with interesting gay men who frolicked at the pool all day. Rehoboth was a hotbed of gay culture, nationally known as gay friendly and, despite the drudgery of the job as a housekeeper, I was part of a scene that was hot and happening and celebrated homosexuality rather than demonizing it.

I worked at Papa John's from ten a.m. to six p.m. and then ran down the boardwalk to jump in the shower, change clothes, and hurry to happy hour at The Palms. The bar was always filled to capacity for the weekend festivities. I walked through the outdoor patio when I entered and was always met with shouts of hello and invitations to join groups of women at their tables. I rarely committed to one seat but grabbed a drink and circulated while I kept my eyes open for good friends or new faces that were worth a second look or an introduction. I was friends with Paige, the bartender, and as soon as she saw me, she knew what cocktail to place in front of me.

The summer of 1988 was filled with pool parties and dinners at wonderful restaurants with groups of women who were new to me. I was given the nickname "Fun Mills" by my new friends, but I missed my life in Maryland and I missed the girl I left behind. I had not asked Teresa to wait for me and she did not. Quite the opposite.

Spending those months in the gay resort of Rehoboth Beach was the first time I was far from family and completely immersed in a gay scene without returning to the straight world every weekday morning. I felt free, no longer confined by or under the control of anyone or any job. But it remains interesting to me how I wanted and needed to get back to the confines of the triple life I thought I needed to escape. I was also anxious to start working in my new position of Assistant Principal and ready to begin the administrative career I had worked so hard to achieve. The triple life had become commonplace to me, so even though it was secretive and hard, that was my life.

By changing schools and getting promotions, I always had a grace period before the new staff members were comfortable enough to start asking personal questions. I tried to be friendly but did not want to make real friendships with the people at my schools. I thought it would be easier to keep a distance since I was an administrator who would be evaluating the teachers. That did not always work because many wonderful teachers were interesting, fun people who spent time around me every day. Some of them did become lifelong friends. It just took a long time before I could reveal, or they figured out, that I was not interested in dating men. By the time that happened, we were close enough that I knew them not to be bigots or racists, so I felt safe.

I spent my first year as a school administrator diving into the job and learning as much as I could about every aspect of instructional leadership, management, and scheduling. I did not have a second job for the first time in fifteen years, but that only lasted one school year. The new position was an eleven-month assignment, so I had the month of July off before going back to prepare for the upcoming school session.

That first July not working, a new women's bar opened in D.C. A young straight woman, Abby, was friends with the guys who owned the bar, and she was aware that they only served breakfast, lunch, and happy hour Monday through Friday. Abby and some of her gay girlfriends had the brilliant idea to open the bar on Friday and Saturday nights as a women's dance club since it sat empty from seven p.m. Friday until six a.m. Monday. Abby knew that once she hired gay, female employees, advertised in gay publications, and, unofficially, changed the name of the bar to Sissy's, she would attract clientele that looked like me. The first time I went to check it out, I inquired about a bartending job.

After working behind the bar for one month alongside one of the brothers, they hired me as the General Manager, and neither of the owners worked another Friday or Saturday night. I took over liquor inventory, hiring and firing bar employees, and counting and depositing the weekend money. A few hot, summer Saturday nights, we closed the street in front of Sissy's, and with a permit from the Capitol Police, hosted block parties with live entertainment and a ten-dollar cover charge. We welcomed hundreds of dancers doing the Electric Slide in the street. I no longer had time to spend money; I just made it and saved it. I was paid $125 cash each night plus the tips I made bartending, which averaged $600 to $700 per weekend. Taking home almost an extra $1000 every weekend actually changed my life by allowing me to invest in more beach property. I already owned one lot in Fenwick Island, Delaware and bought three more in Broadkill Beach, twelve miles north of Rehoboth Beach. The eventual sale of those lots resulted in a much higher level of retirement income and more beach fun.

Things were going very well for my triple life. At Sissy's, Abby ran the door and the entertainment and I ran the bar. She and I hit it off, stole a kiss in the kitchen, and soon she was coming home with me rather than driving to southern Maryland after the bar closed. I worked at the bar every Friday and Saturday night for the entire second year as an Assistant Principal. I was working in the most popular women's bar in town and saw at least six hundred women each weekend. My eyes were always scanning the room for anyone connected to my school. That was natural for me, just like scanning the room of every restaurant I entered to see if any of my students' parents were dining.

There was only one glitch during the time I worked at Sissy's. Totally unexpected, one of the patrons asked, "Aren't you the Assistant Principal at Willow Springs Middle School?" Bravely, I stated, "Yes, I am." She answered, "My mother works in the cafeteria there." I had a huge knot in my stomach and, as I was thinking about what explanation I could give for working at this bar, she disappeared into the crowd.

I worried about that until I got to school on Monday, when I threw back my shoulders, walked into the cafeteria, approached the girl's mother, and said, "I saw your daughter Saturday night at the bar where I work." She shared that her daughter had told her that she saw me. I then told her, "Yes, my twin cousins own that bar and I am working for them on Friday and Saturday nights to save money for a property I want to buy at the beach." She thought that was great and it was never mentioned again. I will never know if the girl outed me or if she was lying to her mother about the type of bar it was.

If I was forced to defend working at a gay bar to my superiors, I was prepared to get the owners to vouch for me. After all, they had never seen such high cash register numbers at the end of any night before the gay women arrived. Also, since the woman who ran the door and came up with the idea in the first place was straight, I could be too. No straight bartender has to go through that kind of worry, the pervasive fear of being caught in the wrong place.

After only two years, the bar was sold to a guy who turned it into a sports bar that catered to men's college sports teams. I did not lose my job and a teacher from my school got a job there also. We were all straight while on duty and the money was still good. However, the teams who came into the bar on Saturday afternoons after their rugby games were of little interest to me. They smelled bad, they were too loud, they drank a lot of beer, and left little or no tips.

The final straw for me was witnessing the teams doing "butt chugs." One guy would partially pull down his pants and allow a teammate to pour beer down his lower back, along his butt crack, and into a beer mug that a third participant held. Someone did drink that beer, but I never stayed in the room long enough to see it happen and I certainly did not ask questions. This lipstick lesbian was not the right bartender for those very kind and flattering but stinky and loud college boys. I resigned and went back to holding one job for the remainder of my career.

The triple life continued at its fullest when I became a high school principal. I thought I was fooling everyone because I am a lipstick lesbian. I could hide well behind my heels, dresses, jewelry, and polished fingernails. I trimmed my nails once to take guitar lessons and as soon as my mother saw me, she asked what I had done to my fingernails. I told her about the lessons and had even taken the guitar with me on my visit. She seemed hesitant to believe that was the real reason for the change. When I bothered to think more about that, I got totally grossed out at what might have been in her head. Was she seriously thinking about lesbian sex and deciding that long nails would not work?

During my ten years as high school principal, there were, of course, ten senior proms to attend. I dressed formally and took dates only twice, once the husband of a good friend and once a gay friend from Rehoboth. I could get away with not having a date because I was on duty and needed to be ready to call the police to haul drunk teenagers away or to call parents with any suspicious activity reports. That working evening was not always conducive to having a date anyway. That was my story and I stuck to it.

One of my principalships was in the same town where I lived. The county boundaries were drawn in such a way that four counties touched the city of Laurel, Maryland. I lived in a different county from where the school was located but my house was less than half a mile from the line. There was good and bad to that situation. I would sometimes see parents of my students in the grocery store just after I had taken my weekend morning run. I did not look my best but it certainly showed them the human side of their principal. Occasionally, it happened to be the liquor store.

My students were not my neighbors but some, who had cars and bothered to find out where I lived, would drive by and call out my name. That was not a bad thing either. I had to be sure my roommate's (wink! wink!) bong was not sitting on the kitchen counter where the students could look straight up from the street level to the blatantly placed water pipe. Though that was not my vice, it would have been connected to me in a way that could have been very damaging to my career. I wonder what would have been worse, using marijuana or being a lesbian.

Even though I was not willing to out myself at work, I was getting braver and more outspoken in non-gay situations. During my forty-three-year career in education, there are four words I spoke that make me most proud. Educators often refer to a phrase that is on tee shirts, posters, or classroom walls. It tells us that the word "can't" should not be part of our vocabulary. It says something like, "Change 'I can't' should be 'I will.'" However, one of my proudest moments is when I said, "I can't do that."

During my second year as a high school principal, I needed to hire a new Dean of Students, who would be my second in command. The first one I hired had not been my choice and was highly unsuccessful at the job. She did not know how to do the job and was a racist. Many of her decisions were unfair, slanted against African American students, and some behaviors were hurtful to my staff. I am protective of all my students and my staff, so I quickly drew the line and followed the procedure to remove her from the position. Fortunately, I was permitted to move forward and hire someone else.

Before scheduling the interviews, my immediate boss, the Assistant Superintendent, asked me to stop in to see him in his office. We talked briefly about the administrative opening and the applicants, but soon I realized the real reason for the invitation to talk was for him to inform me, in person, that I was to be sure to hire a minority, specifically a black person.

It felt like hundreds of thoughts and questions were racing through my mind as I sat there looking at him across his wide, solid wood desk. I remember wondering, *How can he tell me to do that? Does he have the authority to tell me that? Why should I make the other applicants jump through the application and interview hoops knowing they will not be hired? How can I make waves? I am gay! What would my parents do?* I knew my father would speak up immediately and that my mother would listen, leave the meeting, think about what had just been discussed, and then return to talk.

Here was my black boss telling me to give black applicants preferential treatment. I did not think his directive was within the definitions of racism, prejudice, or bigotry but I knew it was wrong. So, I considered his instruction and then said, "I can't do that." He looked startled and asked me, "Why?" I explained my reasons and promised to choose the best candidate for the job, but I also told him, with respect, that if he needed that to be done, someone else would have to do it, even if it meant removing me from my principalship. His face softened and his body language became more relaxed when he replied, "We will do it your way." I had always liked and respected that man but after that day, I loved him and our relationship was stronger and I felt like we had a very special secret.

When I think about that day, I feel brave and proud. It reminds me of when I watched Bradley Cooper and Lady Gaga in a scene from "A Star Is Born." I listened very closely when their characters, Jack and Ali, talked about her songwriting ability. Jack told Ali, "You gotta dig deep into your fuckin' soul or you won't have legs. Tell the truth or your audience will know you're not being honest. All you got is you and what you have to say to people. You gotta grab it and you don't apologize or worry. You just tell them what you want to say."

I had legs that day.

chapter six

COME OFTEN AND STAY LONG

ONCE I MOVED AWAY, I stayed detached from my family because I was no longer relaxed with my mother or my sister. I was afraid of questions they might ask. It felt like everyone had the ability to unsettle me and I know it always seemed like I was on edge, even cranky. I had always been easy to get along with and fun to have around, so I believe. But that changed and, even when I was physically present, I was rarely in the moment. What I was hiding and wondering if I was doing a good job of it consumed me.

Ditching my family while also dodging true love became my approval/avoidance behavior. I played hide and seek in a very powerful way because I wanted them to know but did not want them to find out. Even though I have always just wanted to be who I am, I was scared to death that the world was going to find out and hate me for it. That constant battle of wanting everyone to know and not wanting anyone to know lasted fifty-four years.

When you are in the closet, every moment of every day is a calculated performance–the way you walk, the way you talk, your clothes, makeup and jewelry, the way you look at girls, the way you deal with boys, and what you tell your parents about your day. Pete Buttigieg said some of those things about his teenage years and, when I read it, that was another "that's me" moment.

It was 1978, while living with Laura, when I came out with the words that let my brother know I like girls. He made it very easy because his first wife was having an affair with a woman. My brother called me from California and said, "I have something I want to talk to you about but first I have one question." Naturally, I said, "Okay, what is it?" He asked, "Have you ever made love to a woman?" I quickly thought, *Oh, dear God! Where did that come from and what should I say?* But then, without hesitation, I answered, "Yes." Bob followed with, "Have you made any decision about that?" and I, having practiced my avoidance techniques, answered, "Let's talk about you first."

He went on to explain the sad situation he was in with his wife, and he was trying to understand what he had done wrong. Bob's wife was having a physical relationship with the female half of a couple with whom they were good friends, and his wife was leaving him for the woman. Coming out to my brother became unimportant when his life was falling apart. I was so sad for him, and my heart ached, knowing that he thought he had done something wrong. I wished his wife had found her true self before marrying Bob, but now all that could be done was to support him and convince him that none of it was his fault. I did feel some relief for myself because I would finally have a family member who would understand my truth. Even though a gay woman had changed his life and hurt him deeply, he did not hold any negative feelings toward me. From that phone conversation forward, my brother became my steadfast confidant.

I moved in and out of my parents' lives just like my girlfriends moved in and out of mine. When I phoned my parents, they always answered. I did not always reciprocate. There were several years that I avoided talking to my mother on weekends. I imagined that she could tell through the telephone that I was with my girlfriend and other females who partied together at my Capitol Hill apartment.

My twenty-something self reminds me of Tara Westover in her memoir, *Educated*. She loved her family, as did I, but could not stay around them. Tara wanted the education she was being denied at home while I left to live an honest life that I believed I could not live in Level Green, Pennsylvania. Tara got to the point where she no longer saw Buck's Peak as her home. She cut ties with her father. I minimized contact with my mother. We both experienced self-doubt. Tara came to the realization that she was completely different from her family. I only felt different from the females.

Tara wrote to her family that she was cutting them out of her life for a year until she got a handle on her own life. I was not as courageous as she, so I quietly drifted away. We both wanted our families to change because we were changing. Westover stated that she "finally accepted that she needed to be away from the mountain to live in peace, as well as not feel guilty for taking care of herself over her family." Running away did eliminate some of my guilt simply by being removed. It was easier to bear the guilt of distance than the guilt of homosexuality.

My father wanted me to come often and stay long. I do believe my mother felt the same way, but the discomfort between us was overwhelming at times. Even silence during a television show was comforting when I was with my father. We would laugh together and simply share a glance that needed no words. When we watched television, I didn't feel like we were wasting valuable or quality time; I felt like he was giving me a break from the tense conversation that could ensue with my mother. Sitting next to Mum on the couch sometimes made me feel self-conscious and nervous about what she might ask or say during the next commercial break.

When I did bring girlfriends to visit my parents, they were always welcome, but there was a hesitation with my mother. My father was friendly and accepting to each one, but Mum was wary of a newcomer due to realistic suspicions. I wanted my parents to like my current girlfriend and to include whoever it was in our family. After all, for at least a short time, I thought that was going to be "the one." My father always gave a sincere and welcoming hug and immediately teased my friends as his way of making them feel comfortable. Mum usually tried to accept a new person, but inevitably, asked about the previous girl, in front of the current.

My parents were especially welcoming to my girlfriend, Jessica. She, her husband, and one of her sons wanted to see the city of Pittsburgh, so we planned a Fourth of July trip together. We left Annapolis in two cars because I would be staying longer. It was all uncomfortable and a stupid plan from the start. They stayed in a hotel, but I took them on a tour of the city and they came to the house for the traditional celebration for my father's birthday.

My brother was visiting at the same time and my sister still lived nearby so my entire family met Jessica's family. All went well and I thought the stolen moments between Jessica and me were invisible to everyone. Mum was thrilled that I had a female friend that actually had a husband, so her acceptance was immediate. Though my mother was a very bright woman, she did not see what she did not want to see.

On the other hand, the men in my family did not miss a trick. My brother quietly asked me what was going on between me and Jessica. I told him. I was always honest with my brother because he had accepted my life from the moment he learned about me. Looking back, I should have relied on him to help me come out to the other members of my family. He would have given me great advice and would have had the right words to build my strength and confidence. I have always felt safe in the presence of my brother. His calm but straight-forward approach might have been exactly what would have broken through to my mother.

Most important to me is that my father also pulled me aside that day, gave me one of his big, lingering hugs, and whispered, "You are always welcome here–and all of your friends, no matter what." As the hug uncurled, we looked into each other's eyes with a deep understanding. My only response was, "Thanks, Dad," but I believed we shared an understanding that needed no further discussion. His acceptance was the best gift I had ever received.

When other women guests, those without husbands, visited, I started to see a personality trait in my mother that I never knew she possessed. Maybe it was my imagination, but I thought Mum looked at me and my friends as if she was questioning everything we said or did. She did not smile as much and did not have the warm conversational banter we had always shared. I was self-conscious about how I moved and was careful not to get too close to my friends.

It did not matter too much because before too long, the girl and I would break up and they would never see each other again. My parents met eight different girlfriends in twenty-eight years and each of them disappeared from my life and theirs. There were at least four more significant girlfriends (and a few flings with straight women) in that timeframe but, if we did not live together, I did not take them to visit my parents or even introduce them. How could I expect my mother, who stayed with the same man for sixty-four years, to understand my revolving door? Even though I created it, I did not really understand it either.

One of the girlfriends, who lived with me for a short time, was sixteen years younger and could not keep a job. I had worked too hard in my career to have a roommate who couldn't contribute to the rent and the utilities. Nobody is that cute! So when she was not trying to work, she did all the household chores. She was very good at the cleaning, the laundry, and the shopping, and I had lived alone so could easily afford the living expenses; I just did not want to. When my parents visited, my father noticed her role in the household and called her my "girl Friday." I thought that was hysterical and also believed he was sending a deeper message.

My father, one way or another, always let you know what he was thinking, but my mother was not always outspoken and did not usually stand up for herself to people outside the family. If she was hurt or angry, she kept it to herself, especially when she thought it might cause a disagreement or discomfort. This did not hold true when it came to matters related to my sexuality. Mum was the one who asked the most questions and talked to people outside our nuclear family about the fact that I was not dating men and could possibly be a lesbian.

I heard about my mother's disquietude from her best friend and from a cousin's wife. Both of them approached me and said exactly the same words, "Your mother is worried about you." I knew what was coming and I did not want to hear it but I was polite and asked, "What is she worried about?" The answer: "That you aren't dating anyone." My silent reply was, *I am dating someone, but not a man.*

That made me angry at everyone. They had no right to intrude, and I contended that my mother had no right to talk about me behind my back. I maintained the invisible barrier that seemed to exist in each interaction. I know better now, but I was angry that my mother did not come directly to me. At the same time, I did not want her to bring it up. I guess that was me seeking approval while practicing avoidance.

We were usually a close family and were open when talking through our problems. Friends were often surprised about how easily I could talk to my mother about menstruation or private body parts, but after all, she was a nurse and approached things like that in a very clinical way, so I was used to it and those topics did not embarrass me. That openness disappeared around the topic of homosexuality.

Each of my four family members played an important role in my coming out and in how I felt about my life, accepted or not, as a gay woman. I could not live with the thought of being the black sheep of this wonderful family, but I did not believe they would accept me being a rainbow sheep. The men in my family were my biggest supporters, but I never wanted to be a guy. My father's and brother's attitudes were more "live and let live" while the females seemed to want me to fit into a mold I was not built to fit. My mother was the key player in the saga, and her influence and involvement was usually more negative and interrogative than anyone else's.

My mother demonstrated the importance of strong and close relationships with siblings by maintaining close and trusting bonds with hers. They had all learned to be kind and giving but frugal people who were always available to help each other. When it comes to me and my siblings, we rely on each other equally but for different reasons and different strengths.

Bob, Jan, and Maggie, 1953 and in 2020

Top row: Tony, Nana, Charles
Bottom row: Frances, John, Nellie

My father was an only child, so he had no experience with any sibling rivalry or closeness. Fortunately, Dad became best friends with each of my mother's three brothers. The three bright and successful men were very different from each other, but my father developed a bond with each.

I paid close attention when my parents counseled their dear friend and our neighbor, Mr. Rose, at our kitchen table. J.R., as he was known, stopped by to see his friends when he needed support or words of advice. The topic of conversation was always his son, Scotty. J.R. was worried that his only son might be a queer and even called him a "fag." When J.R. drank too much, my parents knew he got physical with both his wife and his son. It was not many years later that my mother worried about me and started to realize that years of ignoring the possibility of a lesbian daughter would not make it go away. She had heard J.R. call his son derogatory names and knew I could one day be the object of the same prejudice. It might even come from her.

I was never included in those kitchen conversations; I only heard small bits from my mother and nothing from my father. I want to imagine that my father would have suggested that J.R. should just love his son and try to support his choices whether he agreed with them or not. After hearing those conversations, I went into self-protection, knowing that same treatment might be coming my direction, but not from my father.

As it turned out, Scotty was gay, but I was too young to have a friendship with him. My mother never verbalized a connection between her knowledge of Scotty's homosexuality and her suspicions about me. Sadly, she watched J.R. get consumed and finally die of alcoholism, but not before he undid his marriage and his relationship with his son. I am sure my mother watched very closely as J.R. and Scotty distanced themselves from each other. No matter what, she did not want that to happen to her and me. But she did not want me to be gay either, so her confusion and sorrow festered for many years.

chapter seven

I AM MY FATHER'S DAUGHTER

DAD GREW UP AT his parents' knees when they worked in the circus, and he saw all kinds of reckless behavior and various lifestyles, so it made sense that my father would have been more forgiving of mine.

Dad's mother (top row, far right) and father (middle row, center) with their circus family.

My father encouraged and supported every idea I had, whether it was trying to learn six different musical instruments or playing several sports. He supported my drum lessons, telling me I could be the next Gene Krupa and he made a practice drum pad so I could practice at home without a drum. Dad put up a basketball hoop for me in the driveway when I showed interest in that sport. Whether I was good or not, he played every sport, including softball, basketball, golf, and tennis with me. He paid for golf lessons, hoping he would cultivate my interest and develop a partner. He knew my talents more than I did, and I should have paid closer attention.

There was no presumption that I had to be ultra-feminine. Dad unleashed me to be whoever I wanted to be and stretched me in many ways by encouraging hard work and instilling confidence. My father even enjoyed watching when I played football with the boys. I knew my father always had my back and that he would put a stop to any discrimination I was experiencing, if I needed him. When I became a young adult, I could tell that Dad understood my truth when he gave long hugs and looked at me kindly and intently but never questioned me, unlike my mother. Years later, his one-sentence acceptance was the whisper that said it all.

Dad first recognized my wilder, unconventional side. Maybe that was because my father was more of a vagabond from a free-wheeling life. There was no surprise he was that way; after all, he was raised in the non-traditional life of circus performers. My father was an entertainer. He came by that honestly too, because his mother walked the slack wire with her family's acrobatic troupe while his father was the leader of the circus band and played every musical instrument.

During the months when school was in session, Dad's parents sent him to his grandmother and two aunts in Winston-Salem, North Carolina, who raised him. When Dad's mother divorced his father and moved to Pittsburgh, leaving her son behind, his father was still traveling with the circus. Dad never complained about his childhood and remained a good son, even though his mother had abandoned him. He regularly visited his relatives in North Carolina, and he would meet his father in cities where Grandad was traveling. My father treated his mother with respect and did what he could to make her life happy. She had not done any of that for him.

I was reminded of my father when I watched Willie Geist talk about Toni Basil on "Sunday Today." Toni, an award-winning singer, dancer, actress, and choreographer, danced professionally in childhood at the side of her mother, who was a vaudeville acrobat-comedian and who appeared on the Ed Sullivan Show as part of a family dance troupe. Toni's father was an orchestra leader who conducted in Chicago and Las Vegas. Noting the parallels between Toni's early years and my father's, I know Dad would have thrived given the opportunities she had.

Instead, during the summers, my father traveled with the circus from Chicago to the smaller towns east of the Mississippi River. He was not encouraged nor given the opportunity to work on his dance skills. I watched television with my father, and he seemed to look longingly at the dancers, whether it was Gene Kelly, Fred Astaire, or Sammy Davis Jr. It surprised me when the footwork of James Brown and Michael Flatley, Lord of the Dance, mesmerized him. Dad truly might have been his happiest on the dance floor. My heart still aches for him when I think about the hot, dirty cubicle where he welded for Westinghouse, and I wonder if he dreamed of lost opportunities dancing, even show business.

Dad was sometimes a man of few words, but other times he got on a roll and was a very funny entertainer who kept everyone laughing. Dad maintained a full array of alcohol at home, though he never drank. Totally sober, he was the life of the party. It didn't matter who was visiting or what they were doing, my father never made me feel like I was intruding or that I was too young to be there.

Because my father narrowly finished high school, the education of his children was very important to him. I benefited most from that because I was the youngest, and my parents could afford college for me more easily than they could for my sister, and especially for my brother. Straight out of undergrad, Dad wanted me to stay in school until I earned a doctorate. He told me he would pay for all my schooling if I would just keep going. My parents did pay for my undergraduate degree, and I am proud and happy that I earned a fellowship to pay for my Masters. Later in life, I paid for my own PhD but not because he didn't offer.

Dad taught me how to change a tire, he bought me my first softball glove, and never contained me in a gender role. My father made me feel like I was okay no matter what and that I could do or be anything I wanted if I was willing to put in the work. That has stayed with me to this day but, like most of us, I wish I had taken his advice more seriously and worked harder when I was young. He was so proud of my professional accomplishments and visited my schools every chance he had. When my mother and father and their friends sat in the front row at one of my school's assemblies, my father beamed with pride when I was on the stage talking to my students. He stood and waved to the crowd when I proudly introduced them as my parents.

A great listener, Dad gave sound advice and would sit with me as long as it took and no matter what it was. The difference between his attention and my mother's was that she was usually doing something else at the same time. She also paid close attention and gave wonderful advice, but she rarely just sat and had a conversation. By simply watching her, my mother was teaching me how to cook, sew, keep a nice house, and clean and bandage a wound. I was learning from both of them how to take things in stride and not to get overly excited during a crisis. They just took care of business.

I could sit near my dad and watch while he was making something at his workbench in our basement. He, or maybe it was my mother, called it "making sawdust." But his projects, including frames for paintings I hung in my D.C. apartment and a beautiful poker table, lined with green felt and complete with spaces for poker chips, drinks, and cards, were perfect.

If there was any school performance or athletic event after work hours, he was there. He gave up his garage so my senior class could build our Homecoming float there, he shared his carpentry skills as we built its frame, and he sat through every band concert and May Day celebration where I performed every year grades seven through twelve.

When I reached the age of about sixteen, my mother seemed to have something else on her mind, something she wanted to talk about but never broached. There was something bothering her that she was not taking in stride. Many years later, Mum told me that she talked to my father about her concern that I might not like men. I wanted to know what my father said about it and my mother told me that all he said was, "Leave her alone." In many ways, he was my hero. Every time I hear the Mariah Carey song, "Hero," I think of my dad and I cry.

Though my parents loved me and provided a life of security, I didn't have a life of truth. I loved them so much that I just wanted to be a dutiful daughter. What I understand now is that the source of my mother's fear and possible guilt is exactly what caused me to flee my safe, secure, false life. It was impossible, at the time I was coming-of-age, to have anything but a hidden life. I was so afraid of my mother's reaction to my life that I did not allow my father's love and kindness to win me over and keep me closer to home.

Once I moved away and traveled home for weekend visits, I always called from the Pennsylvania Turnpike when I reached Somerset to let them know I was fifty miles away. My father kept the phone by his chair in the living room and answered those calls every time. He always sounded excited to hear my voice and to know I would be home soon. When I pulled up the driveway, my mother always greeted me at the back door and my father left his Lazy Boy and his television to give me a big hug and kiss before I even made it through the kitchen. I loved and missed them so much and could not wait to see them. At the same time, I could hardly wait to get back to my real life. I do not like, and I am ashamed of the person I was then.

My father was nothing but good to me, so disappointing him would give me great sadness and shame. When my first car, an MG they bought me to student teach, finally died at the beginning of my first year of teaching, my mother financed my new car through her credit union. The plan was that I would repay her, not monthly but in larger chunks whenever I saved some money. My parents were careful to make sure I loved the car we chose, a bronze Chevrolet Vega, before we moved forward with the transaction.

I only kept the car a few months and sold it, at a loss, to buy a sports car. My father's comment, that he made to my sister rather than to me, was, "That was a cheap shot to your mother." Those words crushed me, but I never said one word about it and neither did he. My mother had a conversation with me, but I was more concerned about the disappointment I caused my dad. He was protective of all of us, but if you messed with my mother, look out.

It was surprising that Dad did not address his dissatisfaction with me directly. Maybe he thought I would stomp away and never return. After all, I had chosen to distance myself from them and was looking for someone to blame for that separation. Declaring independence from my parents and from my mother's values was my attempt to create something different.

I always had Dad's love, respect, and understanding, but running away from my mother forced my distance from Dad too. I still believe that I hurt him more than I know. Or did he just get it? I never wanted him to feel like my departure was another desertion, like his mother's. He might have known more than I ever thought.

Dad was a gentle soul whose humor and generosity lifted our family. I know my brother, sister, and I had different feelings toward and perceptions of Mum and Dad, which must be true in every family. My brother and my father were so similar that they sometimes competed for control. My sister was very close to my mother and had a much more honest relationship with her than I did. The child's place in the birth order creates some of those differing perspectives. In our family, I received more opportunities and more attention for a few years just because, after my siblings left, I lived with Mum and Dad during their time of highest income and when they were preparing to become "empty nesters."

My father was not a perfect man but, in my mind, he was pretty close. He was not formally educated beyond high school except for the training the Westinghouse provided, but I thought he was wise beyond belief. I told people he was like Abraham Lincoln, self-educated. He seemed to know something about everything, and he could fix anything. I thought that was admirable, but he made fun of himself by saying, "A little knowledge is a dangerous thing."

He did not finish every job he started. Sometimes he did just the minimum to keep my mother happy and to maintain our house. Landscaping was not important. Ours was passable but not special or overly attractive. He did not choose to spend his money or his time on that, but when something was important to my dad, he gave it his all and I always knew that his wife and children came first.

Dad became a member of the Lions Club when I was very young. I do not remember him not being a Lion. He was loyal and hard-working and attended every weekly meeting. He sold fruit cake at Christmas and brooms in the spring to make money for the Lions focus on work for the blind and visually impaired. It was my dad's idea to change from selling fruitcakes (who likes them anyway) to selling nuts. I know that sounds a bit nuts, but my dad found a company named Koeze that sold fancy mixed nuts and cashews in cut-glass decanters. They were delicious, though a little expensive, and had a great profit margin as a fundraiser.

Dad sold the nuts door-to-door, took orders at church, and convinced local businesses to give the nuts as Christmas gifts to their clients. My father had such a great personality and knew everyone in the town, so very few people turned him away when he was working for such a good cause. Dad drove a station wagon at the time and the back of that car was stacked high with boxes of those fancy nut jars.

It sounded silly to me for quite a while until I learned how much money my father made for the Lions Club and how much it helped their philanthropic goal. His nickname became "The Nut Man" and he even carried a business card stating his claim to fame. That was the only business card my dad ever owned. As a teenager, I didn't quite understand the importance of fruitcakes, nuts, brooms, and trained dogs for the blind but I traveled to some of his conventions and dinners, very proud of his work. I joined him when he made some of his deliveries when I was home for a holiday. Every minute in the car with him was quality time and I always watched carefully and noted his kindness to everyone.

As Mark Twain said, "When I was a boy of fourteen, my father was so ignorant I could hardly stand to have the old man around. But when I got to be twenty-one, I was astonished by how much he'd learned in seven years." I never thought either parent was ignorant but, like every teenager, I certainly did not think they were cool. Then suddenly they were very cool so I just watched and learned about hard work and the importance of giving. If I had only been strong enough to share my secret with that wonderful man.

My parents did not have money to donate to any charity, but they could give their time and their hard work and they gave plenty of that. Dad was always a giver and was never interested in spending money on himself. I can only remember him buying himself a few suits the entire time I knew him. Surely, he had more as a young man, but from the age of forty until he was in his nineties, two suits and one tuxedo are all I ever saw. He and my mother got dressed up for the Lions Club events and the tuxedo was taken on their trips to conventions. Dad enjoyed having his three girls choose his clothes and the matching accessories. He did have good taste; he just did not want to spend any money on himself.

Most important to him was taking care of his family. My father stayed in the low-paying job at Westinghouse for his entire working life. He was not a risk-taker when it came to his income. The job was stable and so was he. As a welder, he wore dark blue or dark green work clothes that always had small burn holes in the arms from the welding sparks. I 'm sure his skin was burned too but we never heard him complain about the hot, grueling, and monotonous work.

Once we went to an open house at the Westinghouse plant. I remember seeing the small work area where my father spent his day. Always impressed by my dad, I loved being included in his "professional" life but, even at my young age, I wanted to cry. The aisle where his partitioned-off workspace was located seemed dark and lonely. I wondered why my dad could not wear a shirt and tie to work like a few of my uncles did.

Years later, I learned that the products that my father's division manufactured were small but important parts that contributed to the immense project of providing electricity and power across the country. Then I understood how that could give him a great feeling of accomplishment even within his small contribution. That made me feel better. Because of that, when my father talked about me going to college, there was never a question that I would go, prepare for a professional career, and make him proud. I was afraid that he wouldn't be proud of my personal life, so I wanted to make him proud of me professionally.

Everyone loved my father. He was Uncle Bob, Pap, Bob, Dad, and sometimes "Jocko" to my mother's brothers. We all celebrated his birthdays with great flair; after all, it was the Fourth of July. We invited all the relatives and many friends to celebrate the holiday and birthday with my dad and they all came. We cooked food for days and guests brought dishes to contribute to the wonderful buffet of picnic food.

We moved a chair to the middle of the backyard, and everyone gathered around Dad when he opened his gifts. He gave each gift his enthusiastic attention and thanked each person individually. Dad sometimes wore a crazy wig to entertain the little kids but it made his children, including me, a little uneasy or embarrassed. We thought it was weird, but he was a circus boy and was willing to do almost anything for a laugh.

The guests came early and stayed until dark so we could set off the fireworks I brought from Washington, D.C. or somewhere along the road to Pittsburgh, where I hoped they were legal. Dad made a plywood stand where we set off the elaborate show and he always made sure we had a big bucket of water nearby, just in case. The little cousins wanted to help but needed to earn their right-of-passage before they were old enough to be part of the explosive demonstration. We ate, drank, and were very merry, all in Dad's honor. He always loved that day. We all did.

Dad and Mum could set a dance floor on fire. He was a flashier dancer than she was but Mum never missed a step and followed him perfectly. He probably did the box step or some version of the jitterbug most of the time, but he was also creative and could make any dance partner look skilled, relaxed, and like she was enjoying every move, as a strong leader should. I loved dancing with my dad and miss those dances. I especially missed dancing with my father on my wedding day. He would have been happy for Lori and me.

Except for the situation with the sports car, my father and I never had an argument or a cross word. I enjoyed every minute with him well into his nineties. My dad had worked at the local golf course for several years after he retired. He was a starter at tee number one and also organized the golf cart rentals. Suddenly, Dad did not want to work there anymore. He gave no explanation but I always thought someone must have said something mean about the "old man." Dad worked until he was almost ninety years old so he might have made some mistakes. Maybe Dad was too slow for some young, impatient golfer or got confused once, but I could not imagine what could have gone wrong. Abruptly, he quit the job and never went back.

From that day forward, I thought my father's outlook on life changed. He spent more time alone on his Lazy Boy and he even stopped attending the Lions Club meetings he had always loved. Dad easily gave up the wheel of his own van when we went out to dinner, and he was not as much fun as a companion for my mother.

My parents did continue to go to St. Petersburg, Florida every January and they returned to Pennsylvania in late March, always in time to do their taxes. They had a small place in Gulfport, Florida that seemed to be his happiest time. I often thought he loved the Florida getaway, not only for the weather, but because he was far from the activities in Pennsylvania that he had stopped. I continued to visit them in Florida each year, and we had fun going to the beach at Fort DeSoto for picnics and to dinners at Crabby Dick's, Leverock's, and Campanella's with their friends Dotty and Joe. Both parents loved to see me come and hated to see me leave, but my father always held on a little tighter and longer.

Early in 2008, Dad spent some time at a rehabilitation facility in St. Pete Beach after a pacemaker had been implanted. When I visited, he was not in his room and, of course, my first inclination was to worry. My mother was with me so we went to find a nurse who might have some information about his location. The first attendant we found thought she knew exactly where Dad might be. She said, "Well, karaoke just ended so I'm sure he was there." My head snapped toward my mother and hers toward me as we burst out laughing in great delight.

At that moment, Dad rounded the bend from the community room, saw us in the hallway, and gave a big wave. He was dressed in his Docker khakis, a navy-blue cotton sweater, and some leather loafers. He told us he had just been singing karaoke. Oh, was I sorry I missed that! I was not surprised but was very pleased that he seemed to be his old self again and would soon be ready to go home.

That was his last spring in Florida. Once they got home to Level Green in early April, Dad started to have problems with his balance and fell a few times in the middle of the night. My sister and brother-in-law lived up the street from Mum and Dad were called to help get Dad off the floor. After a few of those incidents, I felt like my dad feared the next step would be consideration of a different living arrangement.

When he fell, he could not get up himself and my mother could not lift him. Moving him was never discussed but I was sure that would come soon.

Then Dad started to have trouble swallowing, and he told my mother that he was "ready to take the big trip." She had no idea what he meant because he had not wanted to travel for several years. When questioned, Dad just pointed to the heavens.

By May, he was in and out of the hospital until serious concerns kept him there. I took him his favorite chocolate milkshake and helped him make the transition to another rehabilitation site. We spent Father's Day celebrating with him outside in the gazebo at William Penn Care Center. Monday night, Dad was very weak and could not swallow and could hardly speak. Mum and I decided to give him one more evening visit before I left town the following morning.

When I kissed my father goodnight, he held me close and whispered, "Beautiful." That was the last word I heard him speak, and probably his last word. With nearly his last breath, he expressed his love for me. And then he was gone.

chapter eight

COMING OUT: IT DON'T COME EASY

I WAS TWENTY-FIVE years old in 1976 and, although this mirrored the rise of feminism and the sexual revolution, gays were largely closeted and called homos or fags or dykes. The creation of LGBTQ was at least a decade away, but plenty had transpired in the gay community in the early twentieth century. Except for the Society for Human Rights, which was established in Chicago in 1924 and ceased to exist in 1925, my birth year, 1950, was the documented beginning of the gay movement in this country with the founding of the Mattachine Society. It was one of the earliest gay rights organizations in the United States.

By the post-World War II era, the advent of the television and the anti-homosexuality crusades, championed by Joseph McCarthy, would help push the flowering of gay culture firmly into the darkness and loneliness of closets. There were hundreds of events, marches, raids, beatings, killings, political battles, and triumphs that led us to where we are. A broad overview of the history from 1950 to the present takes me back to where I was and what was happening with my family, friends, and colleagues while each event occurred. My evolution moved forward with the historic timeline.

I was not quite two years old in 1952 when the American Psychiatric Association labelled homosexuality a sociopathic personality disturbance. My parents had no idea their baby would be a member of that sick group. I doubt if Mum and Dad paid much attention to the APA but I can imagine that Christine (formerly George) Jorgensen, the first person in the United States who was known for sex-change surgery, was in the news and the topic of many adult conversations.

When I started kindergarten in 1955, the Daughters of Bilitis was formed in San Francisco as the first lesbian organization that gave gay women an alternative to the bars. Establishing the organization must have been very courageous in the age of raids on bars and attacks on people who did nothing wrong but just for who they were. My brother had just become a teenager and my family moved into the house my father built on Sunset Drive. As far as I know, our small town was free of arrests like those that were taking place across the country to people just like me.

Though I was reading in 1958, it was not at the level of Supreme Court rulings and I doubt if my parents were paying attention. But that was the year of a landmark Supreme Court decision for LGBT rights. It was the first case to address free speech rights with respect to homosexuality. That is also the year Wham-O marketed the Hula Hoop and I spent many days moving my hips in the circular motion that allowed me to take the hoop from my neck to my ankles and back up again. By the way, the first gay leather bar, the Gold Coast, opened in Chicago that same year.

Gays were being treated unfairly and violently, but it is a relief to realize that many gays practiced peaceful disobedience even when they were not really being disobedient. For example, in 1959, the LAPD was harassing gay patrons of Cooper Do-Nuts in Los Angeles, and they fought back by pelting the police with donuts and paper coffee cups. How civilized.

Rock Hudson, one of the most popular movie stars of his time, was at the beginning of his successful career that spanned from the 1950s to the 1980s until he died of AIDS in 1985. Hudson knew he was gay from a very young age and he understood that "if he wanted to be accepted, the very essence of who he was would have to be edited out of the frame." That essence was not widely known, and he did his best to remain in the closet until his death.

Most gays practiced hiding the essence of who you are, and I began that practice in 1959, the day I realized I liked girls more than my mother thought was normal. That is exactly how it felt when I was a teacher by day and gay bartender at night. My real self was edited out of the frame of my teacher character. Maybe that is what my mother had gone through with Peg and my father. I will never know.

In 1965, while I was in high school enjoying my crushes on Barbara and Miss Martinelli and finally finding my first real girlfriend, lesbian, gay, transgender, cross-dressers, and more groups who were being discriminated against began to band together and fight for rights and recognition. Gender non-conforming dressers were refused service at Dewey's Coffee Shop in Philadelphia. Three cross-dressers and a black, gay activist refused to leave and they were arrested. The black LGBT population organized sit-ins and pickets and later Dewey's agreed to end their discriminatory policies. I had no idea how much I would later benefit from their hard work and suffering.

Starting in the summer of 1967, my high school girlfriend was the only person who knew, for a fact, that I liked girls. Two of her boyfriends suspected, but we did our best to keep them guessing. As you know, that did not work very well.

My college years spanned 1968 to 1973 and all I knew, in terms of activism, were the protests against the Vietnam War. Throughout college, I did not mention my sexual preference to anyone. Though the high school girlfriend was on the same campus, she certainly did not want that cat out of the bag, so I was safe for all four years.

During my sophomore year, 1969, the activist group Personal Rights in Defense and Education (PRIDE) published a Los Angeles newspaper that eventually became The Advocate. It is probably the largest and most well-known gay publication in existence. That same year, police raided the Stonewall Inn in New York City, and protests and demonstrations sprung up all around the country. That event, its Fiftieth Anniversary celebrated June 28, 2019, was the impetus for the gay civil rights movements. Nearly one month later, an audience of more than four-hundred thousand descended on a dairy farm in Bethel, New York for a music festival called Woodstock. The event was billed as "An Aquarian Exposition: 3 Days of Peace and Music." I knew all about Woodstock and the moon landing that summer, but I had no idea what was going on in New York City at the Stonewall Inn.

In my sorority, there were a few girls who we suspected might be gay. I was in the company of other sisters when they talked about the possibility that some of the girls were behaving "privately" behind closed doors. Not that anyone was mean about it or even spread the word openly, but it frightened me enough to stay closeted. I already felt like a phony. Pretending to be straight in the middle of a conversation about someone else being gay caused great internal conflict. I couldn't stand being such a hypocrite.

The first march, now considered the first gay pride parade, was at the Christopher Street Liberation Day in 1970. It was in recognition of the one-year anniversary of the Stonewall riots. I spent that summer in Los Angeles working at Norm's Restaurant on Pico Boulevard and living with my brother and his first wife, who would eventually leave him for a woman. The irony.

There I was, in one of the gay hubs of the country, and all I did was hide. I even lied about a date I had with a black man who took me to the Los Angeles opening of the movie Myra Breckinridge. Anything out of the ordinary, which some defined as white with white and everybody straight, might have brought attention that I did not want. While staying at my brother's home, whom I would soon learn was understanding and accepting of everything and everyone, I even lied to him. I did not fool him but I still lied.

The Watergate break-in to the Democratic National Convention Headquarters took place on June 17, 1972, two weeks after I completed undergraduate school. I could barely pay attention to anything but keeping my secret and suddenly, I was given a fellowship that allowed me to return to the Indiana University of Pennsylvania and complete my Master's degree in one year. So, I returned to the surroundings where I had gone into sexual hiding and that is where I stayed for the next fourteen months.

College Senior Photo, 1972

On June 1, 1973, Maryland became the first state to statutorily ban same-sex marriage. Little did I know that I would be moving to that state and starting my first teaching job exactly four months later. I had no clue what was going on politically. That fall, the American Psychiatric Association made the decision to remove homosexuality from their list of mental disorders, so the same month as my twenty-third birthday, I was cleared of a mental disorder. I was oblivious that I ever had a mental disorder, and then I was a survivor.

The seventies were tough for my whole family. I was floundering socially and still hiding my truth while trying to be independent. Both of my siblings' marriages ended in very dramatic ways. Mum and Dad were told the details of both break-ups and it was a lot to handle. They persevered. The shock of me being gay might have paled when juxtaposed to the details of their other children, but I never seized that opportunity. I continued keeping my secret and believed I was the least of my parents' problems for the time-being.

Harvey Milk became the most visible LGBT politician in the world in the 1970s. Milk was the first openly gay person to be elected to political office in California in 1978. During his speeches, he encouraged LGBT people to "come out of the closet." Harvey Milk was murdered the same year but, as a result of his work and his assassination, thousands of ordinary people did just as he recommended and came out. Inspired by Harvey Milk to develop a symbol of pride and hope for the LGBT community, Gilbert Baker designed and stitched the first rainbow flag.

I remember hearing about Harvey Milk on the news and knew it was the first real public awakening of repression against gays. Famous people can sometimes add credibility to your own personal struggles, but they too needed the right inspiration to come out, and they needed to feel safe that they wouldn't lose their jobs–or be killed. It makes sense that Mum was worried about me.

I was afraid to go to the first National March on Washington for Lesbian and Gay Rights in 1979. An estimated seventy-five to one-hundred-twenty-five thousand gays and their supporters marched, but this cowardly teacher could not risk being seen on television at that event. The 60s and 70s were packed with history, music, revolution, evolution, war, and peace. I floundered through it all with no idea of how to make my way and live my truth.

The first case of Acquired Immune Deficiency Syndrome (AIDS) was discovered in 1981. It was viral, deadly, and contagious. Those adjectives sound way too familiar here in 2021. There was not much more known about AIDS for several years so the high-risk populations, drug users and homosexuals, were the main targets of the discrimination.

Sally Ride, an astronaut and physicist, became the first American woman to fly in space in 1983. I wanted to be her and wished I had listened to my high school guidance counselor, majored in math, and gone to work at NASA. I thought my counselor had said Nassau, and even though I wanted to run away, I really did not want to move that far from Pittsburgh.

During the summer of 1988, while I was living and bartending in Rehoboth Beach, Delaware, activists were beginning to use the initials LGBT. After that summer, my professional assignments added up to a successful and diverse career while each school brought its own gay complications. Whether they were gays who knew me from my other life, straights who wanted to dabble, or one well-meaning friend who outed me to a staff member, I was constantly guarded.

As an administrator, especially after I became a principal, there was more to lose if the community and school system leaders found out about my private life, but at the same time, a greater personal confidence was attached to the authority that came with the positions. I still kept my mouth shut and led my personal life in a private way, but I possessed a deeper conviction about myself and I possessed greater self-assurance than ever. I knew I was in charge, not only of the school but of myself.

Undercover and frightened yet confident and in control was quite a combination to live with while still living the triple life. As long as I concentrated on the hard work that resulted in instructional improvements and student success, that is where staff, students, and parents focused also.

When I started the new school year as an Assistant Principal, I had another clean slate with a new faculty. The second person I ever told I was gay was a teacher, Kate, at that school. I got brave and told Kate that my relationship with a substitute teacher, Connie, was more than a roommate. Just the roommate/substitute teacher combination was complicated enough without the gay part, and it should have remained a secret. In a flash, the strict Catholic rebuffed me because of my homosexuality. Our friendship was over immediately.

I must have been ready to test the waters, coming out by starting with someone from work. That failed effort set me back, but her athleticism made me think she was gay too and in the closet even deeper than I was. That was unfounded and judgmental of me. So, to make myself feel better, I tried to believe that I just got too close to the truth. Now I wonder what she thinks about Pope Francis' support for same-sex civil unions and his comment that "homosexuals have a right to be part of a family." I do wonder where the Pope thinks all homosexuals grew up–hopefully as part of a family.

I was granted a transfer to a high school the year after coming out to Kate, so I had another new start with a different faculty. One exciting thing about new beginnings is that you might walk in any door and find the person that will change you for the remainder of your days. That is what happened at my new school where I met the straight woman who would become my best friend and lover for the next ten years. Jessica was beautiful, stylish, kind, and clearly interested in a friendship with me. She possessed a magnetism that drew me to her instantly. In the beginning, I thought about nothing but friendship. I was living with a girlfriend and Jessica was with her husband and two boys.

When Jessica learned that I was a runner, she tried to get me to run with her after school, but what I thought her running skills would be like intimidated me. When I finally agreed, I learned that our paces and distances were very similar, so we enjoyed many long runs that included long conversations about everything in life–mostly hers. I avoided the topic of my sex life. I learned that she had been in an abusive marriage for eighteen years and I started to realize that she might be looking for someone to treat her fairly and care for and about her. I was in a relationship that was compatible but not loving.

Coming out to Jessica was easy. All she knew was that I was single and living with a woman. One night, when we were at Jessica's beach house together, with her husband and children in other rooms, I blurted, "I am a lesbian and I love you." I shocked myself but Jessica did not seem surprised. After that and when we were not with her family, she made the first physical move and we were off to the races. President Clinton gave us "Don't Ask, Don't Tell," which prohibited openly gay men and lesbians from serving in the military, but also prohibited harassment of those in the closet. At the time, that actually sounded fair to me, so Jessica and I adopted Clinton's agenda.

One year into our affair and after three years at the same school, I was appointed as a high school principal in 1994. Part of preparing to leave my job with Jessica was hiring staff members to fill openings at my new school. Since Jessica had multiple certifications, I was able to offer her a position at my school, and she agreed to transfer and go with me. I showed up at my new school where the message, "Welcome Principal Jan Mills," blazed across the marquee. That giant step in my career filled me with pride and anticipation. I walked in proudly with my administrative secretary and my girlfriend in tow. I still had the live-in girlfriend and Jessica had her husband. One would have thought I was smarter than that.

Another new staff welcomed me, so another clean slate. It was a high-performing school with a strong faculty, so I was ready to boost the instructional program and become an active member of the community. My first day in that building, I had a true "holy shit" moment. A female physical education teacher and coach had set up an appointment to talk to me as soon as I arrived. That meant something was very important to her, so I agreed to talk to her right away.

The second I laid eyes on her, I thought, *Dear God, she's Sporty*. I was not using an adjective, though fitting; that was the nickname the staff at Phase 1 had given her. I recognized her from sixteen years earlier, the days when she played softball on a gay women's league in Washington. Her team celebrated, or licked their wounds, at the Phase after each game, where I was either serving tables or bartending. There was no indication that she recognized me, and I certainly did not mention knowing her. We introduced ourselves as if it were for the first time, and she proceeded to tell me what was so important to her and, I guess, what she thought I could not see.

Sporty matter-of-factly stated that she was a lesbian and was out to the school and the community. She was wearing men's clothes, and it seemed obvious that she had had a breast reduction. She assured me that there was no reason to question, wonder, or be uncomfortable about her. The staff, students, and parents accepted her, and she hoped I would too. Of course, I agreed and appreciated her candor. All I needed to say to her was that I wanted her to assure me that I would never hear about behavior on her part that might be perceived as recruiting students to her side. Of course, I said, "your" instead of" our" side. The coach was so sincere and soft-spoken that I could already tell that our school community would love her. She assured me there was nothing to worry about. She was right and I was relieved.

The country was watching the O.J. Simpson pre-trial and trial for a full year from November 1994 to October of 1995, and I was trying to keep peace in a large high school while students wanted to wear "Free OJ" or "Squeeze the Juice" tee-shirts. Gay news was plentiful too. The Defense of Marriage Act banned the federal recognition of same-sex marriage in 1996. A newsworthy high for gays was when Ellen DeGeneres came out on her show in front of nearly forty-two million viewers, and then on the cover of Time Magazine, but we also hit the lowest of times when, in 1998, Matthew Shepard was beaten, tortured, and left to die tied to a fence. His murder brought national and international attention to hate crime legislation at the state and federal levels.

It seemed like the entire country was listening to the good and the bad. People started to talk more about gay rights and their individual beliefs about those rights and those people. By the time we were into the twenty-first century, there seemed to be a positive turn toward understanding, if not equality, of human rights. In 2000, Vermont became the first state to legalize civil unions between same-sex couples.

I continued to wear my skirts, lipstick, and high heels, and the men continued to flirt so life was good in the secret-keeping world. I grew proficient at cutting people off who got too close to the truth, and I could easily turn a conversation away from my life and toward something related to the work we were doing. I did put out the vibe that personal questions were off limits. One of my secretaries told me I was "secretive." I did not like her choice of words at all, so I merely stated, "Not really secretive, just private." I hoped that sent the message that her comment was too nosy for me. We never discussed that again.

I was comfortable at that school and was making many changes and improvements that the school system acknowledged. As it got close to retirement time, I decided to transfer to another school district for my last three years. An educator's pension is based on the highest paying three years of the last five years that you work. So, I left for the seventeen-thousand-dollar pay raise that would significantly improve my retirement.

Another clean start with a staff that knew nothing about me, or so I thought. During one of my very first days at my new school, one of the Assistant Principals asked me to step outside the building for a conversation. I was confused because I was the principal and was able to have any conversation I wanted in my office, behind closed doors, but that did not satisfy Roxanne. We went to an outdoor courtyard and took a seat at a table that was part of the senior lunch area.

Roxanne told me that she was very good friends with a woman I had known for about twenty years. That friend, Anne, had shared information that made Roxanne think that "we might cross paths in social circles." I knew what was coming but was not looking forward to hearing any of it. Roxanne was about to tell me that we were both gay, no surprise, but the upsetting part was that our mutual friend had outed me to my new Assistant Principal. Without hesitation, I let

Roxanne know that our homosexuality would have nothing to do with our jobs and I was secure that we would protect each other.

My problem was with Anne, who told Roxanne about her new principal before I even arrived and without my consent. The gay code had been broken, and a longtime friend had broken it. Roxanne tried to defend Anne by saying, "It doesn't matter since we are both gay and she just wanted me to know all the good things about you both personally and professionally. Please don't be mad at her." Well, I was, and a conversation with Anne took place very shortly after the one with Roxanne.

From my point of view, Anne was messing with my professional life when I had spent the previous twenty-eight years being very careful to keep it separate from my private life. We moved beyond my hurt and anger because in the end, Anne was right. It was actually calming to have an ally on my staff that worked close to me. Roxanne had been second-in-command at the high school and I kept it that way. She ended up being a very good friend and one of the kindest and most hard-working people I have ever known. She also made it easier to fend off people like a nosey PTA President. Most notable is the fact that only gay people have to address situations like that one. We wear our race and our gender physically but, whether you agree with me or not, there is no outward sign that a person is homosexual unless the subject wants you to know.

One morning, shortly after I joined that staff, I entered the small work room, located in the main office suite, that secretaries and administrators shared. All school employees were welcome in that cozy space but never parents. I had walked in to use the microwave and there stood the PTA President. Before I could ask how I could help her, she blurted, "Well, the word on the street is that the five lesbians are in town." I was familiar enough with her reputation to know that "on the street" meant it came from her mouth and she felt entitled to tell school employees or parents any tidbits she heard, or made up, true or false. We even had a parent that was a columnist for the Washington Post, so I thought I was only two steps away from seeing my personal information in print.

The PTA President was referring to me and the four women who were also new to the staff and had transferred from my previous school. Those women were the best educators and administrators I had ever known so I made every effort to hire them. Without hesitation, I looked the PTA President dead in the eye and pronounced, "Wow, I'm the only one who is not married and I am sure their husbands would not appreciate that." I then added, "I do not pay attention to gossip or people who spread it. What can I do for you today?" Oh, she did not need anything, of course, but she got the message to get the he l out of my work room. She learned to never bring stupid shit like that to me again. Her self-appointed entitlement still brings out the profanity in me, but I did enjoy my indignance.

Eventually, the entire secretarial staff knew about my life. They were more progressive than any staff I had known, and they privately knew all about Roxanne, even though she thought she was safely in the closet. I took them and the women on the administrative staff to my beach house for a long weekend each fall so they could begin their Christmas shopping at the Rehoboth Beach Outlets. We nicknamed ourselves "Seagals." Away with the girls, Roxanne and I talked a little more freely about mutual friends and events we had attended. Trust had been built and my maturity and security had finally evolved.

I retired from education in 2004 and was finally more relaxed about my secret life because I no longer had a job to lose. Exactly forty-four days before my retirement, the first legal same-sex marriage in the United States took place in Massachusetts on May 17th.

For the first three months of retirement, I spent most of my time at my beach house in Rehoboth Beach while I was having the upstairs apartment renovated. I was getting it ready for more full-time occupancy for myself while I rented out the downstairs. During that process Lori and I became great friends, and we spent most weekends, along with her girlfriend, attending happy hours and dining out in Rehoboth. We went for sushi at the Cultured Pearl every Sunday night after the weekenders left town.

By October, I couldn't stand being completely retired, so I went back to work, starting part-time, with Anne Arundel County Public Schools in Annapolis, Maryland. Sunday nights were still special nights at the beach until a full-time opportunity as Director of High School Improvement was offered. For the next four years, I went back to the triple life of straight educator, straight devoted daughter, and gay "Fun Mills" in Rehoboth Beach from Friday afternoon until early Monday morning when I returned to the office. The acceptance of gays was growing, especially in the professional environment in which I was so fortunate to be employed. Working at the Central Office made it easier than working in a school with students and parents but the old habits of presenting myself as straight did not drop away overnight or over the next several years.

While I was continuing with my career, I started work in a PhD program, and Lori was growing stronger about getting herself out of the toxic relationship in which she was embroiled. Finally, on the last day of 2007, Lori was free. She was finally available to socialize on her own, so we spent time alone together and started to move our friendship toward something more. It got complicated at the beach because Lori was still half owner of a beach house with the ex. Also, I was not always sure that her ex accepted, or even understood, that Lori was single. I did my best to be respectful of her feelings but nothing and no one was going to stop the forward movement of my relationship with Lori.

What I thought was a sad and confusing step backward for LGBT in 2008 was that California voters approved Proposition 8 in California, which made same-sex marriage illegal. Fortunately, Prop 8 was ruled unconstitutional two years later. There was one huge and great thing about 2008, that was Barack Obama. President Obama posthumously awarded the Medal of Freedom to Harvey Milk and Congress passed the Matthew Shepard and James Byrd Jr. Hate Crimes Prevention Act. President Obama signed the legislation into law.

Lori moved in with me in January of 2009. We were living in a two-bedroom condominium in Annapolis while I continued working and finishing my doctorate. We socialized more and more with my extended family, and it was completely accepted that we were a same-sex couple. The following year, Lori and I bought a house in Annapolis with plenty of room for guests. My cousins and their children came to visit. We took boat tours, visited historic sites, and had wonderful dinners together. We did all the things straight people get to do their entire lives and then "Don't Ask, Don't Tell" was repealed.

Bikes, Boats, Runs, and Loving Life Together

'Don't Ask, Don't Tell" was finally recognized as discrimination in its purest form. DADT was based on the false assumption that the presence of LGBTQ (the Q had been added) individuals in any branch of the military would undermine the ability to carry out their duties. Because of that policy, thousands of brave service members were discharged simply for who they were and whom they loved. After tens of thousands of letters, emails, and calls from members of the Human Rights Campaign, victory was achieved, and President Barack Obama repealed "Don't Ask, Don't Tell" on September 20, 2011.

The deadly Boston Marathon bombing of 2013 was the source of inspiration for former NBA player, Jason Collins, to come out. He said the tragic event "reenforced the notion that I shouldn't wait for the circumstances of my coming out to be perfect. Things can change in an instant, so why not live truthfully?" Inspiration to live one's truth came from various sources for celebrities who announced their truth over the last few decades.

Lori and I not only proclaimed our truth in 2013 but we proclaimed our vow of "'til death do us part." And years before, I never saw that in the cards for me.

For the gay community, the greatest milestone occurred in 2015 when the Supreme Court ruled that states cannot ban same-sex marriage. That same year, Caitlyn Jenner's coming out was possibly one of the most well-documented and publicized coming-out stories of the decade. Jenner appeared on the cover of Vanity Fair alongside the headline "Call me Caitlyn." On her decision to come out, she stated, "If I was lying on my deathbed and I had kept this secret and never did anything about it, I would be lying there saying 'You just blew your entire life.'"

Instances of anti-LGBTQ violence, such as the Pulse nightclub shooting, inspired "Grey's Anatomy' star Sara Ramirez to come out as bisexual in 2016.

President Obama used his position and his heart to promote causes for many groups who experienced discrimination. He lived with hate and bigotry in his own life. Before leaving office, President Obama appointed the first openly gay Secretary of the Army, and the Secretary of Defense announced the lifting of the ban on transgenders in the military. The National Monument to LGBTQ rights, Stonewall National Monument, was dedicated. Sadly, Barack Obama's second term as President of the United States ended, and all groups who fight oppression immediately and profoundly missed him.

With the inauguration of the new president, the fear of oppression crept back into the lives of the LGBTQ community and many other minority groups. In June of 2017, the Department of Defense announced a six-month delay in allowing transgenders to enlist in the military. One month later, the new president tweeted, "The United States government will not accept or allow transgender individuals to serve in any capacity in the United States military." February 2018, that same president announced a ban on most transgender individuals in the military but the following month, the Supreme Court allowed transgenders to serve in the armed forces.

In May of 2018, I reconnected with my wonderful college roommate at one of our sorority reunions in Pittsburgh. I had not seen her in more than forty years, and it was both peaceful and freeing that I could easily say, "I have a wife." As it turned out, Marianne and her husband have owned a house in Rehoboth Beach for several years and we never saw each other there. Now we get together regularly and are both thankful that we will not waste any more time.

Gay identity, as both a personal and political category, did not fully emerge until the mid-twentieth century (exactly when I was born). The term "gay" appeared as an underground term in the early-20th century and came into popular usage in the 1960s (exactly when I had my first girlfriend). It was historically used as a broad term that encompassed the entirety of the modern LGBTQ initialism.

Difficulty existed in finding and openly practicing a distinct lesbian identity because gay women experienced exclusions in both feminist and gay organizations. Betty Friedan, the first president of the National Organization for Women (NOW), referred to lesbians as "The Lavender Menace" suggesting our presence would hinder the goals of the organization by furthering the assumption that all feminists were man-hating lesbians. Now, not NOW, many members of all genders and ages are proud to be known as feminists.

In *A Brief History of the LGBTQ Initialism*, (June 9, 2018) Jeffrey Iovannone states that lesbians often experienced overt sexism in post-Stonewall gay organizations such as the Gay Liberation Front (GLF) and the Gay Activists Alliance (GAA). Gay women were not welcome in many gay organizations or establishments because most were owned and run by gay men. I witnessed gay men treating gay women with disdain when we entered their bars or restaurants. Many gay men did not care for the women who dressed like boys and acted manly.

Being a lipstick lesbian was a little easier, but once three friends and I were almost refused entry to The Renegade in Rehoboth Beach because the man at the door thought we were straight and coming to gawk or make fun of the queers. When we did our best to assure him that we were gay, he pointed to one girl in the group and actually said, "She's too pretty to be gay." I was not sure if I should laugh, punch him in the face, or walk away. Since I had never punched anyone in my life, and never will, we just walked past him and entered. Of course, three of us must not have been too pretty to be gay. How rude!

Eventually, each finds his own incentive to come out. Some find it very late in life, too late to share it with the most important people. I do feel like I blew many good years with my parents by staying in the closet. What I did not know was that they would live another forty years. I wish I had had the courage to take Harvey Milk's advice.

If you are struggling with coming out or if you are a parent who does not know how to handle the coming out of a gay child, be aware of what those who came before have gone through to give the LGBTQ community the rights and freedoms we have today. Hopefully, some of this information can suggest what not to do to young people.

Through my writing, I am suggesting a pathway that allows those who are gay or in an unhappy relationship to be open. My hope is that my writing journey releases others to be true to their own selves. I was not and I learned the hard way.

We all have the right to love who we love.

Janis E. Mills

chapter nine

COURTING STRAIGHT GIRLS

I HAVE KNOWN STRAIGHT people who were afraid of gays because they believed homosexuals have crushes on or desires for every member of their chosen gender. That is just like saying every straight woman is attracted to every straight man and the same for every straight man to straight women.

Some straight parents fear gay educators because they make unfair assumptions about what might happen between the teacher and the student. The anxiety, from the teacher's point of view, is that the parents might come to the school and tell the administration they do not want their child in a certain teacher's class. The parent fears what the teacher could do to the student physically, or that the teacher will instigate a change within the student. You know, "make him queer." More and more, children are announcing to their parents that they do not identify with their given genders, and school administrators are dealing with trans kids, new pronouns, and even teens having gender reassignment surgeries. These are all important and relevant changes in our culture, though we still live in a heteronormative society.

Homosexuality is not contagious nor is it a choice. We cannot turn you into one of us. Knowing and living all that, I still had the conversation with Sporty about recruiting. I doubt if I was really worried about the students; my greatest fear was likely that the word of homosexuals on my staff would implicate me. That connection made no sense, but nevertheless, it was real.

Some homosexual teachers continue censoring themselves by not talking about their weekend activities or by changing the pronouns they use to describe their partners or even their secret spouses. Often, teachers are forced to make a choice: "Do I reveal my truth or do I protect my job?" Then along comes the straight parent who flirts with the gay teacher and ends up having an affair, leaving her husband, and remaining in a long-term relationship with the teacher. Yes, it happens, and it did with a friend of mine. The child, a high school senior who knew exactly what was going on, begged her mother to wait until after graduation before flaunting her love affair with the teacher. The mother refused, came out publicly, and she is still in a relationship with the teacher. So, there are extremes in both directions, but as a gay former teacher, all I wanted was my privacy and the freedom to teach.

During my sixteen years as a school administrator, every case of a teacher being accused of inappropriate behavior toward a student was a straight man making advances toward straight girls. That is not a blanket statement of truth in the world; it is only my experience. Of course, bad behavior exists with all genders and all preferences. My focus is women and, specifically, the conundrum of attraction between straight and gay females. I have had seven of those encounters. Some became physical and the others were bonds of almost inexplicable strength that came within a hair of a kiss or even more.

The Journal of Personality and Social Psychology published an online article on October 26, 2015 that highlighted a study on getting in touch with female sexuality. The University of Essex study researched 345 gay and straight women and measured the arousal of women using eye tracking devices and direct measures of physiological sexual response. The study stated that "gay women tend to be exclusively sexually attracted to women, while straight women are more likely to be aroused by both sexes. Only 28% of straight women were mostly aroused by their preferred sex, compared with 68% of gay women." The study concluded that no woman is "totally straight." It also stated that the sexual arousal patterns of gay women are much more like men, whose responses tend to accurately mirror their stated sexual preferences. Dr. Gerulf Rieger, who led the study, concluded that "When it comes to straight women and sexual arousal there is such a disconnect between what a woman tells me and what her body does."

What impact do these sexual responses have on friendships? In some cases, they are simply part of our connection as friends. Many straight females are tempted by gay women. It must seem so safe. Is it really cheating on your man if there is no penis involved? Sexuality is very personal and sometimes consenting adults, along with experimenting teenagers, enjoy exploring various kinds of sexual activities. Straight people have been known to have flings, crushes, or full-blown affairs with gays. There are gay women who find chasing straight women thrilling. I am not one of those women.

Women usually feel safest with their friends, but since I did not grow up in the era of the "hook up" culture, I did not face any straight-to-gay encounters until I was in my forties. Oh, except for my high school girlfriend, the one who left me for the guy she has been with nearly fifty years. I guess I have to count her as straight. I certainly thought she was gay at the time, and she did make the first move. That is important. She is also the reason I changed the names of most of the women in this book. After all, we were kids, but I would bet that her husband still would not be able to handle it.

When the sexual tension emerged in some relationships I had with straight women, I did not know, and did not think about, the fear of rejection on the part of the friend. For her, it was probably complicated with the fear of being a lesbian or being perceived as one. Every straight woman I had sexual relations with told me that she was not a lesbian and that the attraction to me was the only physical attraction she ever had to a woman. The "I'm not gay, it's just you" comment was very flattering, but I did not believe that for one minute. Perhaps I was the only one she acted upon, and that was flattering too.

Remember, Greta Garbo even had homosexual affairs and called them "exciting secrets." For me, it was the straight affairs that were even more secretive than my entire gay life. It took a long time before I talked about liaisons with straight women to my lesbian friends. I did not look at those dalliances as conquests, but I imagine my friends thought those flings were hot. Sometimes, I heard the question, "Why mess with straight women? They can have all the men they want, and they do not deserve us."

When I first arrived in Washington, D.C., I had no idea how to take the first step into a relationship with a woman. Friendships had always developed with ease, but once I was away from Pennsylvania, it was time to go ahead and try to be more obvious about my intentions. Before I knew where to find gay women, I met new friends at work or through straight friends. Those were not optimal for romance, but I now know that I started to behave differently toward women who attracted me. Exactly as it happened in high school, eye contact was held a little longer and the gaze was deeper. During conversations, I listened with great intent and took my fixed look away before it became uncomfortable. I posed questions that implied interest but did not get overly curious and certainly not flirtatious. The intention was to leave her wanting more. I did not realize it at the time, but that must have been my covert manner of flirting.

Claire, also a teacher, became my friend the moment we were introduced. She had a great sense of humor and was very bright, feminine, and attractive. Soon I thought I had a secret crush on a straight friend who did not have similar feelings. We had great fun together when we shopped, went out for happy hour, carpooled, and even drove to visit her parents when her husband was not available. She taught me how to use chopsticks and introduced me to Ledo's pizza, a lifelong treasure.

I spent a few Saturday nights with Claire and her husband, Ronnie, at their Capitol Hill row house. She and I loved to cook and we made delicious dinners of fresh seafood from the Maine Avenue outdoor market while her husband selected the music and poured the wine. The three of us were great friends, but I always felt guilty about my feelings toward his wife.

Ronnie helped Claire choose her first softball glove so she could participate in the faculty softball games. She had never played the sport before, and her husband was baffled but supportive. After one of our games against a rival school faculty, and after a few beers, she revealed that she only played so she could spend time with me. She also revealed that she told her husband that I was her soulmate. I never understood why he was not her soulmate. There was that wonderful woman laying out the truth to me and I didn't give her a shred of encouragement or declare how I felt about our friendship. In actuality, I wanted to steal her from her husband and never look back. That was not possible, so I remained stoic.

After more than a year into our friendship and with no warning, Claire told me that she "had to stop seeing me because she was starting to feel closer to me than she was to her husband." I was shocked, I could barely speak, and I did not try to explain that she could have us both. I knew she could not. That bombshell told me that she was in deeper than I realized. I was too afraid to say anything like, "Doesn't that tell you something about yourself?" I did not fight for the friendship and, once again, a straight girl broke my heart. Almost as quickly as it started, it ended.

I am not sure what I expected. I did want her to be attracted to me and she was. I did not want to break up her marriage and I did not. I did know the friendship could not stay the same and it did not. So the self-fulfilling prophecy just hurt both of us. That was a full-blown break-up and ruined what should have been a great and enduring friendship.

Several weeks after no communication with Claire, she wrote me a letter expressing how upset she was and how she missed our friendship and the love we shared. I was astonished when I saw the letter and confused by both the content and the fact that she would put such intimacies in writing. I did not reply because I could not believe there was a way back to our friendship without hurting her marriage and I could not be a part of that. I knew I wanted more but I had to walk away.

Like the line from John Grisham's, *The Rainmaker*, I thought, *You must be stupid, stupid, stupid.* Maybe I was–or maybe I was smarter than I remember being in my twenties. The attraction game we played was dangerous and hurtful, but I cannot honestly say that it never happened again. I thought straight friends were safe, especially if they were married, and that there was no harm in getting close to the line we should not cross, but thankfully, I did learn from that second heartbreak and never landed in that place again.

Abby, a straight girl who changed our bond to a physical one, had a boyfriend who she eventually married, just like my high school experience. I didn't think about it then but maybe being with me sent the two of them running back to their boyfriends! Abby was the woman in charge of the door and the music at Sissy's, the bar I managed in Washington, D.C. She was very attractive, and I noticed her the first time I walked into the bar. I inquired of the cocktail waitress if they were looking for a bartender and she sent Abby over to talk to me. Since she was working there, my friends and I presumed she was gay. I was single, open to new prospects, and my friends told me to "go for it."

Once I started the job, I found out that her boyfriend was helping set up the music. That was a disappointment, but he left after the bar opened and did not return until two a.m. to give Abby a ride home. She and I had plenty of time to play and she was a flirt. We had a lot of fun bantering and laughing throughout every Friday and Saturday night. We shared little side stories about the women in the bar, did Sex-On-The-Beach or Kamikaze shooters together, and sang with the music when we were cleaning up and counting money at the end of the night.

One night in the tight quarters of the ice room, Abby stopped, looked at me, and kissed me right on the lips. That was fine with me. I had nothing to lose, and I felt in control of the exciting secret–just like Garbo. Abby talked to her gay friends, who also worked at the bar, about her attraction to me. They encouraged her to "go for it." That seems to be a common theme when friends are talking about matters of the heart that have nothing to do with them.

Since the bar closed so late and the closing chores took an extra hour, Abby and her employee friends started spending Friday nights at my house, trading their hour-long drive to Chantilly for a seven-minute drive to Cheverly. We slept until almost noon and only had a few hours before we had to get ready to go back to the bar anyway. It was a lot of fun, and one night when we were all sitting around my kitchen table at four a.m., Abby stood up, reached out for my hand as she looked into my eyes, and calmly asked, "Are you ready to go to bed?" I was ready to go to bed.

The next week, she told her boyfriend she needed some space and was moving into my house until she figured out what she wanted. He knew I was living alone in a three-bedroom stone cottage not far from Sissy's, so Abbey's "time out" was acceptable to him. Abby and I enjoyed our time together playing house, and she was pretending to be my girlfriend but in a sly way. We both knew how it was going to end, but we were big girls and trusted that one would not hurt the other. That was very different for me, because once someone moved in with me, I usually thought it would be a forever thing. The fact that we both knew it would eventually end made our connection seem mature and spontaneous.

After a few months, we knew it was time to part. Abby realized a life with her boyfriend was her truth and that was what she wanted. She did tell me that he did not meet all her needs, which I had figured out early on, but that she did love the kind and caring man he was and she did want children. We remained friends, still worked together at the bar on Capitol Hill, and she stole kisses occasionally in the same ice room. She was sad when I started dating someone else but honestly, and for a change, I had to take control of my life. I do not understand it when women end relationships because they choose another person and then get upset when the one they left finds someone else. Human nature can be hard to comprehend.

My new love interest, using the word love very loosely, was sixteen years younger than I, and once again, it did not last very long. Some women who taught at my school had become my friends and knew all about the destructive young thing who was living at my house. They were protective and came to my house, joined by my neighbor Cory, as back-up when I kicked the youngster out.

Cory was straight and taught high school science in the same school district as me. We had become good friends as she watched me closely for a few years and became interested and curious about my gay life. Her best friend had been a gay man, who sadly committed suicide while Cory and I lived across Tot Park from each other. He was a southern, military man who could not live with the secret he held and the disappointment he would cause his family if they found out he was homosexual. Cory talked about her best friend often, but only shared that he was gay with two people. The two she confided in were also gay. I wondered why she made that choice, but I also thought it might be because Cory's situation was the same. She was not military, but her father was, and he would not have accepted her as gay.

One night, after Cory had a few beers and we were alone at my house, she professed to be "the straightest person you will ever know." Then she kissed me, took my hand, and led me into my own bedroom. I got a good laugh out of that, but I kept the humor to myself. She thought she was serious and even reminded me of her straightness after our frolic in the bedroom.

It must be the alcohol that ignites the attraction to gay women in some straight girls. Cory left a party at Andrews Air Force Base one night, of course with many men, and drove to see me where I was the principal of summer night school. She was clearly too intoxicated to drive or to be in my school, so I tried to walk her to her car to wait until my work was finished. She stopped in the middle of a secluded hallway and tried to grab and kiss me. This was a completely different person from the respected, professional woman I saw in our neighborhood.

Cory was a good enough friend that she threw a surprise party for my fortieth birthday and invited members of my school staff and other friends. She and I also worked together at the bar that took over Sissy's location after it sold and became a straight sports bar. It was not long before I left the job at the bar and Cory moved to a townhouse community about five miles away. She started climbing the ladder in the school system, working at the Central Office while I continued to get promotions too. I saw Cory when I went to meet with the Superintendant or to attend principals' meetings. She was always happy to see me, friendly and interested in my career and my life.

I moved on to a new school district and it was not too long before Cory was dating one of the guys that worked in her building, and soon they were engaged. Once she was married, it seemed as if she was totally freaked out by what we had done, and she needed to erase me from her life and her memory. I guess there was no full disclosure in the relationship with her new husband.

I have seen Cory exactly three times in the last nineteen years. Twice were in my school district and once at the mall across the street from where I live. She said hello, but when I walked away and then turned back to say something else, I caught her rolling her eyes in a mean way, sending some message to the woman she was shopping with. My feelings were hurt, but I felt sorry for her even more. What we had was a good friendship that included a one-nighter. My assumption is that she was not able to maintain the friendship because I was her secret and she did not trust me to keep it. The friendships we throw away for the wrong reasons still make me sad.

Finally, the last straight woman I messed with was the one with a husband. Jessica and I saw each other in a romantic way for almost ten years. She and her husband had a house in Rehoboth Beach before I bought mine four blocks away. I truly did not buy the house or choose the location because of her. I had loved the town for many years and was ready for an investment close to the ocean.

After seeing me on the side for five years, she moved out from her husband, supposedly as the precursor to being with me. Her husband had demanded that she move out of Annapolis, where they had lived for several years, because it was "his town." Since I was living in Annapolis also, I was not pleased that she moved almost thirty miles away. However, she did choose a town closer to the school where we both worked. The commute from her townhouse was short and fast but the inconvenience of going back and forth with clothes and my dog created a hardship that soon outweighed the excitement. That sounds shallow and was not the only reason we began to grow apart.

Jessica started to have great anxiety over leaving her home, even though the circumstances with her husband were unbearable. She self-prescribed drugs and her anorexia became even worse than it had been for all the years I knew her. We tried to enjoy our time together, often going to my beach house, but her mental state started to take a physical toll on her and was a great strain on our partnership. She would disappear for hours, out walking with her dog or taking my car to visit a palm reader (for real). It got crazy, and my family noticed the bizarre behavior when they visited me in Rehoboth.

My brother found Jessica in an upstairs crawlspace sleeping in her underwear. I tried to help her, but when she was alone in my house and set the microwave on thirty minutes instead of thirty seconds, the firemen had to be called and I lost all patience and attraction when I saw that she, literally, almost burned down my house. I cried when I saw the blackened walls but was also relieved that the damage was not permanent and she was not hurt. I loved Jessica, but I had to admit that we could never make this work. I had spent years waiting for her youngest son to graduate from high school because that is when she said she would leave her husband. Finally, when the time came to finalize the divorce, Jessica was the one that could not bring herself to sign the papers. I was finished.

Jessica moved back to her husband, who had become her good friend. They lived more like a brother and sister than a married couple. I saw Jessica's brother once after she and the husband sold their house on the water and moved to downtown Annapolis. Her brother knew exactly what Jessica's and my relationship had been, so he told me that her mental state was not good and that I would never have my friend back.

It was devastating losing Jessica while also a kind of relief. I wanted her at my side, but she was not comfortable being there in my gay world. I had worked too hard and fought too long to go back into the closet with her. I could not backtrack in my effort to reveal my truth. It was not like I wanted to win any straight girls over to my side. I just wanted to be with women I was attracted to and even when love prevailed, deep inside I knew it would not be long-lasting, would likely end, and would break my heart. You just cannot change a person, especially her sexuality. Heartbreak number three from a straight girl.

Fortunately, I had a dear friend, Mary, who watched as Jessica left the husband and as she returned to him. Mary and her husband were always there for me, and I could call and go to her house without notice. I loved her and depended on her, and she felt the same way about me. There were no games, no kisses, no flirtations, just honest and deep friendship between one straight and one gay woman. So, it can happen.

As is true in many women's friendships, sexuality, jealousy, and competition are often commingled yet not openly discussed. Even today, the issue of sex and friendship between women can still disturb. Author F. Diane Barth wrote in her book, *I Know How You Feel: The Joy and Heartbreak of Friendship in Women's Lives*, that Christina Aguilera says she is straight but finds women "hornier to look at" than men. That is similar to the findings of Dr. Rieger in his study I mentioned earlier. Dr. Suzanna Rose, a researcher specializing in the psychology of women's relationships, says that love and friendship are "two discrete yet inextricably intertwined concepts, each relying on the other for full expression." I agree.

Janis E. Mills

chapter ten

REHOBOTH BEACH–MY SAFE HARBOR

IRONIC TO ME BECAUSE of my Methodist upbringing, Rehoboth Beach, Delaware was founded as a Methodist Meeting Camp in the 1870s. Deep into the twentieth century, one of my straight girlfriends attended Episcopal retreats at the original Methodist building while the town was attracting visitors from within Delaware but also Washington, D.C. Those visitors increasingly included gays, especially men. Both legislators and their staffs poured into Rehoboth and the groups included quite a few gay people.

Rehoboth folklore has it that the oceanfront DuPont property was where Rehoboth's gay nightlife began. Tallulah Bankhead is said to have been one of the guests while the local art league welcomed a group of women painters known, in addition to their artwork, for their close camaraderie. Now it makes sense to me that Tallulah's grave is in Chestertown, Maryland. If she was hanging out in Rehoboth Beach, only seventy miles away, she might have had roots in the area.

In the 1950s, long before I stepped foot into the town of Rehoboth Beach, The Pink Pony, where gay men gathered for happy hour, opened on the boardwalk. In those days, revelers were not permitted to carry their cocktails as they walked around the bar so the scene would have been much different from the happy hours of today where the men and women move from table to table, joining in conversations and maybe never sitting at all.

A decade later, The Pleasant Inn and a few other guesthouses in town enjoyed a word-of-mouth reputation of being gay-friendly. When The Pink Pony was destroyed by the great 1962 storm, about twelve miles south along the shore, Nomad Village had opened. The hotel and bar complex catered mainly to gay men. There were small A-frame cottages behind the main building and groups of gays also rented them and gathered at the bar and the outdoor pool.

Word spread that the back room of Nomad Village was a great meeting spot for closeted folks from D.C. Approaching the hotel from the main entrance along Route 1, just north of Bethany Beach, one would find the registration desk for the hotel and might not have a clue about what was happening and who was partying in the secluded bar. Just like most gay establishments of that time, the clientele was mostly men, but gay women were welcome and straight hotel guests also shared the pool. When the pool started to fill with the gay men and women gliding down the sliding board into the pool and squealing while playing games with beachballs, the families usually headed to the beach only one block away.

I spent my share of days frolicking in the Nomad pool and enjoying cocktails from the outside bar. Nomad Village was open for nearly thirty years until the A-frames became affordable tiny houses, before they were called tiny houses, and as they sold, the property shrank and the gay visitors had fewer rooms for lodging. Nomad Village closed in the '90s, but by that time, there were several gay bars and restaurants that replaced it only a quick drive north on Route 1.

In the 1970s, my parents went to Rehoboth Beach to visit their friends Peg and Howard, who had a house in the Country Club Estates area of downtown Rehoboth Beach. Rehoboth's reputation as a traditional family resort continued while more and more gay visitors arrived. My mother did not especially like Rehoboth because it had too many queer men. Those were her words, and she made the exact same declaration about Key West. Of course, that piqued my interest in the cozy beach town at a time before I even met the gay girls that I would later vacation with on the coasts of Delaware and Maryland.

Later in that same decade, I was living only one hundred twenty miles from that little oceanside village, and I rented beach houses with friends in Fenwick Island, Bethany Beach, and Ocean View. We always drove the fifteen miles north to Rehoboth Beach where the Blue Moon and The Renegade were exclusively gay restaurant-bars and there was an openly gay community. Straight people were not exactly unwelcome but back then, most straights were not comfortable in the company of large numbers of gays. In my opinion, there were many straight-by-day men who visited both establishments on the "down low."

My friends and I spent weekends saluting the disco era at The Boathouse in Dewey Beach, one mile south of Rehoboth, where a German Shepherd protected the property by pacing on the roof of the building at the bay end of Dagsworthy Street. The Renegade, a disco bar, offered raised dance platforms, private cabanas that surrounded the pool, an outdoor bar, and a Ladies Tea Dance every summer Sunday.

You could see women in everything from tank tops and athletic shorts to starched blouses, capris, and heels.

The lipstick lesbians were well put together and acted as if they had just rolled off the beach looking that good. Others that jumped in the pool had no makeup to worry about and went straight to the bar or the dance floor after toweling off. It was always jam-packed, and after a few drinks and dances, I usually headed to a great restaurant for fresh seafood and nice wine with a group of friends. The unfortunate partiers who worked Monday morning headed north on Route 1 toward their hometowns. Even when I worked full time, I stayed Sunday nights and drove home at five a.m. on Mondays. I would do anything to avoid ruining a good Sunday night at the beach.

While the girls spent Sundays at the Renegade, hundreds of gay men gathered on the beach at the south end of the boardwalk at the appropriately named Queen Street Beach. The boys nicknamed their out-of-the-way beach Poodle Beach and it holds that name today. The guys celebrate Memorial Day every year with drag volleyball at Poodle Beach. It is a sight to behold. Each volleyball player is in full drag and the crowd of revelers includes everything from formal drag attire to muscle men in thongs. The crowd has grown over the years with the acceptance of homosexual humanity. The massive crowd, that now includes gay boys, girls, and some straights, surrounds the court in the sand and is so deep, you can barely see the game unless you arrived hours early and staked your claim on a prime spot for your beach chair.

The Blue Moon opened in 1980 and immediately brought a bright blue and yellow restaurant to a neighborhood that was beginning a renaissance. Gay men still gather in the bar and on the front deck for happy hour, and the restaurant has won accolades from straight visitors and gay and lesbian couples. Live music fills the Blue Moon on summer evenings and a line forms along the sidewalk of Baltimore Avenue once the bar has reached capacity.

In 1981, The Washington Blade, a gay newspaper, printed an article about the increasing numbers of gay vacationers, gay bars, gay restaurants, and gay businesses in Rehoboth Beach. The locals feared that the information might harm the family image of the resort town. Then, driven by word of mouth in the gay communities of Washington, Baltimore, Philadelphia, and Wilmington, the gay migration to Rehoboth continued to swell.

The movement coincided with a new era of gay pride, disco, coming out, and increased activism following the assassination of

Harvey Milk in San Francisco, and the anti-gay tirades of Anita Bryant in Florida. The gay proliferation in Rehoboth Beach was about to make the town another stop on the summer circuit of gay resorts along with Provincetown, Fire Island, and Key West.

I fell in love with Rehoboth Beach in the mid 1980s and started spending most vacations and the entire summer of 1988 in the town that gave me freedom and privacy only two hours from my super-straight role as a school assistant principal. I got to be well-known around town. After all, I became "Fun Mills" there. The friends I made in Rehoboth were from Washington, D.C., Baltimore, Philadelphia, Wilmington, and many small towns that surrounded those cities. I was able to socialize with those ladies from my homes in Cheverly and then Annapolis, Maryland, and many of them remain my friends today.

A disco named The Strand opened on Rehoboth Avenue, smack in the middle of town, that same summer. Hundreds of gays and a few straights danced under the disco ball and a select few climbed the winding staircase to the VIP room that overlooked the dance floor. There were rumors, but I never knew for a fact, about what happened in that room. By the early 1990s, a clear and concentrated effort to get rid of The Strand grew rapidly among some property owners and some townspeople. The concern about parking and noise was mentioned but that was not enough for the city council to vote for the removal of the business.

Some city leaders decided to recommend that bars not connected to restaurants be banned from the downtown area. Since The Strand did not have a restaurant, it fit that unwanted category. For that fabricated reason, the bar was denied a liquor license. It seemed to be a clear case of discrimination, but in my opinion, it worked for some of the straight folks. A bar and disco without liquor was not a draw for the fun-seeking gay crowds. The Strand closed. It was fun while it lasted but there was always an uneasy feeling for me when I entered. The dancing was great but a bar with no alcohol felt like it could be a front for something different, so I danced elsewhere.

CAMP Rehoboth, an acronym for "Create a More Positive" Rehoboth, was founded in 1991. It remains a non-profit group of LGBTQ volunteers who work to bring all people in the diverse communities of Rehoboth Beach together. That has always been at the heart of the CAMP Rehoboth philosophy. The history of common bonds built between straights and gays is thanks, partially, to CAMP Rehoboth. The city's real estate boom that united gays and straights in the mutual quest for nice houses, a nice community, and nice profits continues to evolve.

The house I own in Rehoboth was purchased in 1995 and it sits one block from the ocean and three blocks from the hubbub of Rehoboth, Baltimore, and Wilmington Avenues, where most of the gay action still takes place. Thankfully, it is not really just gay action anymore. Any given event might be predominantly gay or straight, but most happenings, restaurants, and bars are gender and preference mixed. You can see drag shows at the Purple Parrot, which is predominantly a straight place, and you will witness straight couples dancing and comfortably mingling with queers at The Pond and all around town.

There has always been a relaxed feeling of freedom and peace for me in Rehoboth Beach. Crossing the Chesapeake Bay Bridge, headed east to Delaware, there was always a release of tension when my mind would finally open the closet door that restrained me through the work week. I use past tense because I don't need that release anymore. The openness of that beach town now exists for me almost everywhere.

I knew purchasing my beach house was going to be a lucrative investment. I had already purchased four building lots in Delaware and was counting on them to increase in value, which they did. I learned to "buy low and sell high." But the main reason for the purchase was to have a fun place where my family and friends could gather and vacation.

For several years, I rented the downstairs, three-bedroom unit to weekly vacationers. I blocked out weeks for family to stay there and it was a wonderful spot for cousins and their families to come and enjoy the beach and the family camaraderie. My sister and her family brought their friends, who traveled in a huge RV. We parked the vehicle in the driveway, and I cannot even tell you how many teenagers came with them.

The RV started draining the power from the house to the point that it tripped the circuit breakers over and over. Fortunately, my brother was visiting at the same time and he was able to work some magic I cannot describe with the electrical capacity of the house. All I know is that soon there was an additional circuit breaker box in the basement. Most important was that everyone was happy, and I was able to share my safe harbor with family and friends who, I still believed, had no idea I needed to be safe. I 'm sure that joke was on me.

My mother and father came to stay with me a few times. Some of my best memories are times with them at the beach. One of my favorite photos of my mother is her sitting on the white, wicker settee on my upstairs, screened-in back porch. The fabric on the cushions was seashells in various shades of blue on a butter yellow background. My mother's soft, summer pants and shirt were narrow blue, white, and yellow stripes (very coincidental) and MaddieRose, my fawn rose and white whippet, laid beside her while she read. They look so happy and peaceful, exactly how I felt when sharing my home in Rehoboth with them.

I cooked for my family and we went to fun restaurants together. One of my friends used her four-wheel drive Jeep to drive us onto the beach above North Shores so my parents could sit near the water without walking too far on the sand. My parents were in their late eighties but were still spry and great sports. They were willing to try any new adventure, especially if their children were included. So, we piled onto the beach with our blankets, folding chairs, and coolers. We enjoyed the beach for about thirty minutes when a fast-moving summer storm drove us back home. That storm just added to the memory and we laughed as we got soaked piling all the beach paraphernalia back into the Jeep and making our quick getaway.

My socializing and choice of restaurants changed when family was visiting. The double life took over and I pretended to be straight in my gay town. Of course, I didn't take them to any bars anyway but I also steered away from the restaurants where someone would call me "Fun Mills." Even though the nickname was a good thing and had no hidden meaning, I did not want to explain anything to my parents, especially my mother.

Mirroring the way my parents said they felt when I visited my childhood home, I loved it when they arrived and felt great sadness when they drove away. To make it easier, I would usually organize the trip so that we left together, and all stopped in Annapolis for at least a one-night visit before they headed back to Pittsburgh. I believed it was easier to say goodbye to them when I was back in the less fun but more stable environment of the town where I worked.

After many years of men owning gay establishments, except for the Blue Moon, a group of women got together and opened a bar and restaurant that specifically catered to gay women. It was small with not much of a dance floor and I cannot remember what the menu offered or how the food tasted. It must have been unremarkable, but it was important to support the only female-owned women's business in town. The Beach House was located on Rehoboth Avenue and had all the right components to make it a success.

Ladies packed the bar on Friday and Saturday nights May through September, but the remainder of the year brought small crowds and little income for the owners. Women's hearts are in the right place when it comes to supporting women-owned businesses, but female incomes remain significantly lower than men's, so trips to the ocean and nights out become expensive and out-of-reach for many women. After trying to stay open year-round, there just was not enough business to warrant the expenses of our only getaway. After a summer or two, The Beach House closed.

Just like any resort town, some businesses in Rehoboth close after one year, many fold after five seasons, and some become iconic, like the Blue Moon. What we can count on is that CAMP Rehoboth will continue to thrive and to organize events that attract large crowds of gay men and women to the town. Sundance is a two-night event on Labor Day Weekend, which includes a silent and live auction, cocktail buffet, open bar, and a dance party. Families Weekend, Women's FEST, LGBTQ Film Festival, and LGBTQA+ Youth Circle continue to attract gay singles, married couples, and families throughout the year.

The LGBTQ events welcome all couples and families and continue to foster common bonds and unite straight and gay people of all ages and ethnicities. We enjoy Drag Bingo at the Convention Center, where drag queens host the bingo night that has become so popular that there are rarely seats available unless you arrive early and save a seat. North Shores continues to be a popular beach where gays and straights commingle, unlike the days when the gay women congregated on the right side of the jetty, the men went to the left, and no straights were seen unless they accompanied gay friends or family.

The girls' side of North Shores beach was crowded with women of all sizes, shapes, colors, and interests. Some threw footballs while others threw mimosa and Bloody Mary parties. My friends and I strolled up and down the beach and stopped by each blanket or circle of chairs that included friends or new acquaintances. You could buy a mango slushy at the tiny concession stand and, sometimes, we just happened to have a small bottle of vodka in a beach bag, ready to enhance that slushy.

I did then and still enjoy lounging on my second-floor deck. From one block back, it has a limited view of the ocean but a perfect view for people-watching. Both straight and gay couples, individuals, and families wave and say hello as they pass. They notice the two adorable dogs on the deck and secondly notice the humans. Many times, I wore the skimpiest bikini I owned and would lie on the floor of the deck so no one could see me. It was fun listening to the passersby comment on the adorable cottage and the cute dogs on the deck.

President Biden owns a second home in Rehoboth Beach and frequently parks on our street when he attends Sunday mass. We have been fortunate enough to share morning greetings with both Bidens while walking down our street, and we have seen them at the Henlopen City Oyster House. I had the opportunity to talk to Dr. Jill Biden and to Hoda Kotb at their book signings at Browseabout Books on Rehoboth Avenue. Maybe they will stop in to see me one day at my book signing.

Joe Biden has parked his dark green Corvette, a gift from his son Beau, directly in front of my house. He does not know that we guarded it as closely as he would. A male gay couple, who previously lived next door, held a fundraiser for Joe Biden's Presidential Campaign at their new home four blocks away. And one Sunday, when he was leaving his church, I called to the then former Vice President from my front porch, saying, "Hang in there, Joe. We're with you." He waved and quickly walked toward his car. He hung in there and it has worked. I can uncross my fingers, thank God, and do everything I can to support our new President.

I think of Rehoboth Beach as my town. The town and I have made tremendous strides in the forty plus years that I have been going there. My town has turned out to be open to same-sex hand holding and open conversations between all humans about your wife or husband no matter your gender, preference, or race. I watched closeted school employees with high-ranking positions hide in the back of the Blue Moon, and now they are openly displaying their wedding rings at the open-air happy hours at Aqua.

My safe harbor was not just for me but has been that safe place for many gays for many years. Now I am happy to see that safe places exist for all of us almost everywhere.

Janis E. Mills

chapter eleven

MY WIFE AND OUR LIFE

AFTER LORI'S PREVIOUS RELATIONSHIP ended on New Year's Eve of 2007, we began spending more and more time together, and we took all of 2008 to move away from being just friends. My father died in June of that same year, and Lori joined me traveling back to Pittsburgh for his funeral. I wanted her at my side even knowing that, at the age of fifty-seven, we were going to present as a couple in front of my family. Finally, I did not care. This meant my mother would realize what she feared was true.

Lori and I were relaxed being together and her support and attention made it clear to my family that we were together as more than friends. It was interesting and almost fun to watch the veiled glances and hidden whispers that rippled through the group of relatives. Maybe the nature of the event helped but Lori was warmly welcomed and accepted as someone they knew they would see often. My cousins were wonderful and seemed to take my unspoken but public outing in stride. I do not think my relatives are stupid or naive but that is exactly how I had been treating them. They had seen through my secrecy for years and I appreciated their respect for my privacy. It was so much better to have that door finally open.

When that long day ended and we had finally settled in at my parents' house and changed into our pajamas, I sat beside my mother on her bed. While saying goodnight, she handed me a photograph of my fourth-grade class. We looked at it together and giggled at the dresses with round collars all the girls wore that emulated our mothers' fashions, the slacks and tucked-in shirts for the boys (no jeans were allowed), the neatly combed or slicked-back hairdos, and the innocence on all the little faces. Then the bomb dropped.

I had been waiting decades for one of us to finally blow my cover. My mother's comment was timely, planned, and masterful. She handed the school photo to me and said. "Take this upstairs and show it to your sweetie." That was it. My mother had just outed me for me and freed me from my façade and any future lies. My eyes filled with tears as I kissed her on her soft and warm cheek, but all I could say was, "Thanks, Mum."

I later realized how coincidental it was that my mother used my fourth-grade class photo from school year 1959-1960, the same year I was eight years old and ran into the kitchen asking, "What's a queer?"

I would have thought I would be jumping for joy when I realized my mother understood my relationship with Lori. I was stunned, but juxtaposed to my father's death, I was not ready to celebrate. Instead, it was anticlimactic. That should have been the moment of an explosion of happiness for me, a celebration of acceptance. I wish we had talked, shared, hugged, and started a deeper understanding of each other. We never did have that conversation, but it was good enough to finally know I was accepted and loved just as I am.

Mum liked Lori very much, and soon grew to love her and to expect her to be with me every time I went home to visit. Once Mum knew about Lori and me, I did not care what anyone else thought. I finally realized that the more Mum knew about me, the more we could really dig deeper into lurking secrets and layers that we both had been hiding. Out and free, I still grieved for the time we had lost and all I could have shared with my father. One great thing about my mother's few words was that I instantly jumped from the triple life back to the double. I continued to hide my gayness from colleagues, but I was open everywhere else. In hindsight, it must have been almost silly to those smart and observant co-worker friends.

The January after Dad's funeral is when Lori moved in with me in my beautiful, two-bedroom condominium in an Annapolis community, walking distance from the city dock. We started our forever life, and my love for Lori also included relief that we were finally together and enjoying a time when my mother could visit and share our joy and our truth. We anxiously awaited the day when our country would recognize our right to love.

I was making the transition from being single to having a partner and Lori was transferring from one partner to another, letting go of ties to the ex, working through the joint custody of two pups, and embracing a new relationship with me. We had fun rearranging the space where I had been living alone for ten years. I was using every inch of the ample space–for one. So, I emptied the walk-in closet in the second bedroom, not an easy task, to accommodate Lori's belongings. We redesigned the closet, adding shelves and racks while moving the large items like golf clubs and skis to a storage compartment. I never rented a storage unit before because I believed those spaces were full of junk. If I need or want something, it must be important enough to keep close by. I learned that from my dad.

I made an exception for Lori because I knew it was temporary and the storage unit held items we did want and did need but could get along without during our time of sharing the small condominium. I packed my summer clothes into boxes and bins and transported them to my beach house for the winter months. Then, when spring came, I did the same with my winter clothes. Even with the second closet available, it did not take long to realize that the closet space was barely sufficient for two working women who took their appearance seriously.

Lori brought a large chest of drawers with her, and it fit into the walk-in closet that had become all hers. We both folded, stacked, or hung each piece of clothing in a way that was the most compact and efficient use of space. The second bedroom had always been an exercise and tv room so it remained the same with a leather fold-out loveseat, a treadmill, and a large 1990s version television. I had also moved my mother's library table, one where she did her homework when she was a child, into that room, which also served as my study room during my PhD program. I was nearing the end of my course work when Lori moved in with me, but I still had another three years of study, research, and writing my dissertation ahead of me.

Lori had never witnessed how much time I spent reading and writing papers, so we needed to develop routines that would accommodate both of us while allowing quiet time for my academic work. My workday began at eight a.m., so I started getting out of bed at 4:30 to spend a few hours focused on the work for my final course. I went to class one night each week, usually a Wednesday, and did not get home until nine. When I finally walked in the door after a very long day, dinner was ready, a glass of chardonnay had been poured, and Lori was waiting for me. She had taken my whippet for her final walk of the night, so I was able to drop my books and briefcase, take off my coat, quickly change into pajamas, and sit down for a delicious dinner with my girl.

Lori had a thirty-mile commute to work every day so, on my non-class days, I tried to have dinner on its way to being ready when she got home. We always exercised, so a long walk or a trip to the gym was also part of each day. Our habits slowly melded into one life for two rather than individual lives. The transition from living alone to having a full-time, live-in partner was courageous and powerful. I was overjoyed and getting comfortable with someone other than just me coming home to the condo every day. Coming home to me. I finally believed that I could relax and enjoy our life together. I trusted the relationship was going to last the remainder of our lives. We were both content and in love. At age fifty-eight, it was a feeling I had never experienced.

During the cold months of our first year together, Lori and I started taking hot yoga after work on Fridays. Our routine was to complete the yoga, stop next door to pick up sushi, drive the mile and a half to the condo, shower, pour the wine, and cuddle up on the living room couch in front of the television. We watched an episode of "Friday Night Lights" before crashing at the end of a tiring week. We truly loved the coziness of the condominium and the closeness of our new relationship. Cooking together was entertainment for us while we sipped our different but favorite wines, or the occasional cosmopolitan or dirty martini.

We enjoyed our weekends thoroughly, but I always had to incorporate time to study for my comprehensive exams that were coming up in October. I completely took over the second bedroom as my study room by sticking large, thirty-six by forty-two-inch posters up on every piece of uncovered wall space. Each poster was covered with the information from one course that would be covered on the comps. Every detail of each course had to be in my brain and ready for the transfer from brain to paper during the eight-hour exam that was spread over two days.

Lori was totally supportive and helpful throughout that stressful time. I do not think I made the bed or washed one load of laundry during the three years of comprehensive exam preparation and dissertation writing. She did everything while allowing me to focus on my work. That way, when I could get away to have some fun, the household chores were complete. Every day, I learned more about Lori's giving and caring nature. By living together, we had the opportunity to dig deep into the details of each other's character and I definitely liked what I was learning. I hope she did too. I guess she did; she is still here.

While I was working on the doctorate, as if I was not busy enough, Lori and I decided we needed more space, so we started house hunting. We looked at many locations in Annapolis; most were houses that were already occupied, but we soon realized that buying someone else's dirt was not in our plan. We were specific about what we wanted in terms of size and creature comforts, but location was most important. No, most important was the gradual and strong bond we were building and how comfortable I was with my family and their acceptance of my life.

Only one mile down the road from the condo, a new development called Monticello was going in, and it was walking distance from a few restaurants and boutiques, our gym, and the coffee shop we frequented. It was also close enough to walk to the city dock of Annapolis, but it would be more of an exercise walk than walking to one of the restaurants or shops. We loved everything about the development, and we finally chose our favorite model and were fortunate to acquire the largest lot in the community. We signed the papers in September of 2009, taking a giant step in our relationship.

During my non-study hours, we had a wonderful time choosing all the accessories and fixtures for the house. We visited the design center and chose all the details for the kitchen, bathrooms, and flooring, and the timing for the sale of the condo worked out perfectly. I felt like we were playing house and needed to remind myself that this was real and life was finally good. Yes, world, two women bought the house and two women were choosing the furnishings and getting ready to live in it–together, forever. The profit from that sale allowed us to choose beautiful furniture to augment the pieces from the condo and from Lori's collection that we wanted to incorporate into the house that was three times the size of the two-bedroom unit we left.

Our families were thrilled for us. Lori's mother, sister, and my mother visited the first weekend, which was also Lori's birthday.

The guest rooms were furnished, so we welcomed them and were proud to give them the tour while explaining the plans and dreams we had for our first home. The birthday celebration was planned at a favorite, local restaurant, but just before walking out the door, there was a small problem with the plumbing. That small dilemma ended up being an overnight fiasco until the builder could send in a repairman to undo the damage workers had done by throwing soda cans down a hole in the bathroom floor before the toilet was in place. I had never heard of such a thing happening.

Not only did our wonderful dinner turn into Chinese delivery, but I had to go next door, introduce myself to our new neighbors, and ask if my ninety-three-year-old mother could use their bathroom. They were wonderful and even offered to leave their downstairs entrance unlocked so we could go in and out any time during the night if we needed to use their facility. That is one way to make friends. They remain some of our best friends today.

Celebrating our new house–Lori (reclining), Sylvia (Lori's mother),
Nellie (my mother), Me, and Amy (Lori's sister, standing)

Lori and I were comfortable in our new home like I had never been before. There was a different feeling, knowing I would be with that person until I die, and I was able to talk about those feelings with my mother and others close to me. Lori and I talked a lot and shared ideas and opinions about everything. We understood each other because we communicated about everything and compromised when needed. I had never argued before in a relationship and I had a hard time getting used to having small disagreements and understanding that it was okay. It actually feels more honest and real when every thought and idea you have is not perfect to the other person.

Closeness to both families, especially our mothers, is important to us, so we traveled back and forth to Pittsburgh or to Lancaster for most holidays and several weekends.

Mum and Sylvia celebrating Mother's Day 2015
Lidia's Restaurant in Pittsburgh

Lori and I handled family problems together while keeping our relationship as our primary focus. I was not accustomed to having someone prioritize me while I also prioritized her. Even though I had owned two previous houses with two different girlfriends, there was never the feeling of peace and permanence like the one I had when moving in with Lori. I bought the other girls out of the houses, they moved out, and I moved on. That will never happen again.

With Lori, it is different, and I attribute that not only to our love, commitment, and maturity but also to the fact that I was out to my mother and would never lie again about my living arrangement or sharing a bedroom. It felt exhilarating and it was life-altering. Lori and I often mention that we wish it had happened twenty years earlier. How wonderful that would have been! But, trying to think about the present, we are grateful that we are finally accepted as normal people in a real marriage.

chapter twelve

ENJOYING WHAT LIFE WAS SUPPOSED TO BE ALL ALONG

I HAVE SHARED LESSONS learned and mistakes made throughout my life. Not that I will stop learning or making mistakes, but I finally believe I have evolved enough to let down my guard, practice total honesty, relax in my truth, and enjoy life as it comes. I hope some pearls of wisdom might also be gleaned from the great or the mundane happenings after my mother helped me come out to her. I now tremendously appreciate family events that come naturally to straight people because they did not happen prior to June 21, 2008, the day of my father's funeral.

My mother lived alone on Sunset Drive after Dad's death, two days after Father's Day. She had frequent visitors who included my sister, two cousins who live only one quarter mile up the street, and many other relatives and friends. Mum had a large circle of people who loved her and each one wanted to make sure she was not lonely. I know she had her vulnerable moments, but Mum stayed busy with various sewing or volunteer projects.

My sister was wonderful about stopping by every day on her way home from work, and dinner was usually shared at one of their homes. My cousin, Josie, who has always been like a younger sister to me, still lives up Sunset Drive from my parents' house and stopped by often for tea, to bring Mum treats from Schramm's Farms and Orchards in Harrison City, or just to say hello and check on her. Josie is a registered nurse, so it was comforting to know that she was checking on my mother's mental and physical well-being during each casual visit. I envied the time my mother shared with Marge and Josie.

Finally out and comfortable with my mother, I still prioritized everything else even when she needed me most. I was working full time three hundred fifty miles away and was trying to spend as much time as possible with Lori, developing our new relationship. I regret that I did not do something differently, and Lori would have agreed to anything I needed to do for Mum. After all, I had retired in 2004 but decided to go right back to full-time work in a different county for the next twelve years. The twenty-twenty vision of hindsight tells me that was not necessary.

It was not long after my father died that Mum allowed my siblings and me to reconfigure some rooms in her house so she could remain on one floor. Her laundry room had always been in the basement and her sewing room on the second floor. We converted my old bedroom on the first floor to a laundry and sewing room, Mum's bathtub was changed to a walk-in shower with a seat, and my brother added a second handrail to each stairway. We knew my mother would find reasons to visit the upper and lower levels no matter what we did, so the safety precautions were installed.

Lori and I loved our weekends on Sunset Drive. Every minute with my mother was more relaxed and enjoyable than visits had ever been. Truly, ever. I was no longer keeping secrets and worrying that my facial expressions revealed my urgency to leave. Lori and I always found fun things to do with my mother and anyone else who would join us. We took Mum and her cousin, Anne, to the North Hills of Pittsburgh to have lunch at a diner we saw on Guy Fieri's show "Diners, Drive-ins, and Dives." We took her shopping at Dick's Sporting Goods or any place where she could get a motorized cart to ensure her independence in the store. She lost us and had a blast zooming up and down the aisles. Mum loved buying Lori and me each a Steeler jacket. She had to make sure we remained steadfast fans. No worries there.

Mum was using a cane in the house but moved to a walker when we went out. She continued to dress up, fix her hair, and apply light make-up and lipstick when we went out to dinner. She started to choose lower, more comfortable shoes than previous years when we made the short treks to DeNunzio's in Monroeville, Atria's in Murrysville, Parente's in Trafford, or Olives and Peppers in Level Green. We always preferred the Italian restaurants even though we are not Italian. I asked my mother if the mailman was Italian. She just laughed, knowing Italian food was always my cooking specialty and my eating favorite.

My mother was still able to travel, so my sister brought her to stay with us every time Marge visited my niece, who was living only eight miles away from us in Annapolis. The family togetherness and the acceptance of my true life was something I had never experienced in the first sixty years of my life. On Memorial Day weekend of 2012, Marge brought my mother to Maryland to join us for my PhD graduation celebration. Lori and I, our mothers, two of our sisters, and one good friend rode together, in a limousine Lori had hired to the ceremony at Baltimore's Convention Center. Mum used only her cane and was so proud of my accomplishment and excited to share that day with all of us.

PhD Graduation Day: Lori, Mum, Me, Maggie, Diane, Amy, Sylvia

Mum was attentive and clapped and cheered when I crossed the stage. She laughed and told stories in the limo on the way home, acting at least ten years younger than her chronological age. Graduating from Notre Dame of Maryland University with my PhD was celebrated surrounded by my family and Lori's, another event that most folks take for granted. I never expected to be able to include both families and behave like a real couple in front of everyone. We took at least twenty friends and family members to the Severn Inn in Annapolis for a celebratory dinner. I gave a short speech and thanked everyone for their parts in my success. I especially gave credit to my wonderful partner who, almost literally, dragged me through the final years of the comprehensive exams and the dissertation. For those who take family celebrations for granted, I highly recommend you take a good look at how fortunate you are.

Two months earlier, March 1, 2012, Maryland Governor Martin O'Malley signed same-sex marriage legislation into law, a move that an overwhelming majority of voters approved. By New Year's Day, 2013, gay couples were allowed to have legal matrimony. Lori and I went ring shopping the next day, and what fun we had. It was interesting watching the jewelry store employees react to the fact that they were selling two identical engagement rings to two women. Doubling the value of the sale might have helped with the acceptance of a same sex couple, if they needed any assistance with that.

We were in a financial position to choose whatever rings we wanted, and we really went for it! I wanted Lori to have a ring she was proud to wear, and one that let her know the depth of my love every time she glanced at her ring finger. We decided on matching rings, which is the only time I agreed that we should be "matchy-match."

It took a few months to relax into our new roles as fiancées and to be prepared to wear our rings in the world outside our gay circle. We felt legitimately engaged in May and I wore my engagement ring into work, where I had served as the Director of High School Improvement for the past six years. That was a place where only a few people knew I was gay. Though I was brave and proud that day to show off my new bling, I was also slightly nervous. As soon as I saw the first member of our team, I held out my left hand and said, "I have something to show you." That dear friend and colleague immediately shrieked with delight and called to the other team members in the office to come and see my two-carat diamond flanked by eight half-carat stones.

Without mentioning a pronoun for my fiancée, Janine said, "Show us a picture." The group was well-aware that I never mentioned any men in my life. But I also believed that most of them had no idea I was not straight. When I pulled up a photograph of Lori and me on my phone, I heard a few gasps and Janine said, "You two are gorgeous!" That second, I was so grateful for her icebreaking approval. She had no idea how much those few words meant and how they helped me get through my big reveal. Then we all started to cry. Of course, when I was met with this immediate, emotional support, I wished I had told them years earlier.

That scene evokes a lesson I can share with anyone who is shielding their sexuality from colleagues or friends or family members. Whether you are twenty or forty or sixty-two, like I was at the time, you are wasting time. Learn from my mistakes. All those decades I was in hiding, I was often lonely, and sneaking around never feels good. Flaunt it and be proud, like I was showing off my diamond. You also have a burgeoning LGBTQ movement behind you, a community that I never had while coming of age, and into my truth.

It was time for my triple life to end. For too many years, I had dressed in business suits and dresses for my educator roles that spanned from teacher to principal, then rushed home on weekends to change into tight jeans and starched, white shirts to sling cocktails at gay bars on Capitol Hill. I added eye makeup, red lipstick, and high black heels–like Clark Kent in the phone booth, a change of attire meant an unleashing of a person, one who did feel super and more powerful in her new, authentic role.

Lori and I both had some difficulty with our families when announcing our marriage plans. My mother had just gotten used to the fact that she had a lesbian daughter–now this! I did get some pushback from her. As soon as our engagement was official, I called my mother, sister, and brother. Mum tried to sound happy, but her voice was soft and halting. She quietly asked why we wanted to get married. I told her, "For the same reason that you and Dad took your wedding vows and wanted to spend your life together. Lori and I want to be together forever and we can finally, legally, make our love official."

In later years, my cousin, Josie, shared that my mother confided in her that it was not so much the engagement announcement that rattled her. She was most upset that our upcoming marriage meant we were going to start having sex. As a strict Methodist, Mum had warned me since I was a teen that sex before marriage was a sin. What was she thinking? That here I was, a daughter who was a senior citizen, and Lori and I had just been platonic roommates for the five years we were living together?

Lori's family already knew she was gay, but she chose to share the big news of our engagement in person–that was long before Zoom. Lori did not want to tell her mother that we were engaged over the telephone, so she waited until we were visiting her family in Lancaster, Pennsylvania. We had just gotten our God fix at a huge concert hall with evangelist Joel Osteen, so we were feeling spiritually righteous and strong.

When we stopped at a restaurant after the service, Lori's sister, Amy, pointed to Lori's ring and asked, "What's that?" Lori's mother, Sylvia's face underwent a series of quick changes, from a slight smile to jaw-dropping disdain. She had seen Lori, her oldest daughter, in several short-lived, same sex relationships and perhaps she did not trust that I was the one with whom Lori could go the distance.

I was sixty-two and Lori was fifty-two, and we were not asking anyone's permission to be wed. We also did not expect joyful acceptance with open arms. What we did expect was that they would be happy that we were happy. It was not until the wedding that we both did feel that they truly supported our choice. We knew it was right, that we could say "I do" and believe that we could sustain our bond. Lori knew she wanted a marriage far different from her parents, and that I would be a stable partner. I trusted the institution of marriage, inspired by my parents and many relatives who were examples of lifelong love and commitment.

Most of all, it was the strength and resilience of the women in my family, who endured many tragedies and much loss, yet had the willpower to carry on. My maternal grandmother, Nana, watched the earth devour three family members in her backyard. My mother saw that horror and carried a dim memory and the inherited trauma her entire life. Mum observed her mother raising five children alone and penniless, making ends meet as a midwife and a seamstress. Nana had been married to my grandfather for nineteen years before he died, another example that provided confidence in the institution of marriage, but theirs was suddenly and drastically ended.

Nana and My Grandfather's Wedding Photo, 1901

Dad's mother, Gram, was forced to leave her home when she was only ten years old to perform in a circus with the family acrobatic troupe. She walked the slack rope, she balanced on a pole that her brother, who was walking the rope, held, and she performed various floor acrobatics. She was the pregnant bride of the leader of the band by the age of seventeen, a man with whom she stayed married for twelve years and bore one child.

My mother inherited her mother's strength. From the average number of childhood pranks, teenage late nights, and even car accidents, my siblings and I escalated our disappointments to unplanned pregnancies and finally a girl who liked girls. Nellie persevered. Because of the formidable female ancestors, I learned how to hold fast to my convictions. Yet looking back, I wonder why I was too weak to share one of the primary aspects of my life. I thought I was comfortable in my own skin, but my armor of flesh was not comfortable out in the world where homophobia prevailed, and I felt safer to continue the straight charade.

But today, if you are afraid, it is a good time to be bold in your convictions and trust that your loved ones will still love you, even if they do not support your lifestyle. You are in a new generation of persons embracing gay relationships and coming out against the backdrop of a more forgiving society. Though our culture is still heteronormative, it is shifting quickly as colleges are offering majors in queer studies, and openly gay celebrities and politicians, from Ellen to Pete, are proud and out. Check out the marriage announcements; they always feature same sex marriages.

I often think about my devotion to my mother and why I am re-examining that love. I needed to dismantle the unrealistic version of her that I held in my heart. The real version is enough to idolize. I admired so many of her qualities and I watched closely when she treated everyone with great gentleness and compassion. She administered allergy shots to neighborhood kids and adults who could not afford to go to the doctor, and she made our house the favorite stop at Halloween by making her homemade candy apples. Following her example, I quit my job soon after my mother died so I could spend more time with family and more time helping others. I thought I loved her so much that I wanted to pick up where she left off. Five years after her death, I reflect on this. How could I have blindly revered Mum when I know now that she really did not know me?

As Soren Kierkegaard stated, "Life can only be understood backwards; but it must be lived forwards." I clearly waited too long to examine my life, my relationships, and lessons from my mother and father. But now all these regrets and would-haves, should-haves are spilling out of me, with two goals: to unburden myself and celebrate the present and to help others. The last thing I ever wanted to do was to disappoint my parents. At my expense, I lived a false and often lonely life.

My parents cannot be disappointed now, and what I can do is help open doors for another generation of parents and of young gay people who, despite the evolution of LGBTQ acceptance, may still be fearful of showing their truth. It took too long for me to declare my independence from my parents and their respective values to flex my own.

Reflecting on my mother's reactions to my sexuality, I realize that there were likely secrets that she held too. Secrets that affected her deeply. I do wish I had known years ago that when my mother talked about her fear and embarrassment of possibly having a homosexual daughter, she too likely had a crush on Peg, the woman with whom she lived in her twenties when they were both in nursing school. This I will never know.

By the spring of 2013, Mum was getting more forgetful and repeating herself more than ever before. She started to make some mistakes in the house, like pushing the wrong button on the microwave and heating her coffee for three minutes, which resulted in a bad burn on her hand. My sister started to get very concerned about Mum living alone, even though she was still driving at age ninety-six. My brother took her for a test drive and agreed to approve her skills if she promised to limit her trips to the grocery store that was three miles away and the hairdresser, less than one mile away. I was skeptical.

Marge and her husband talked about making changes in their house to accommodate my mother, but no adjustments were going to make it comfortable for all of them and safe enough for my mother. That is when we gradually started inserting some conversations about assisted living. Mum agreed to stay at William Penn Care Center in Export, Pennsylvania for one week when Marge and her husband were out of town. Mum actually enjoyed the visit because she knew several people who lived there. However, a one-week visit was far from agreeing to move to William Penn permanently. The care center was about eight miles from Mum's house, so that was the post-retirement home of choice for many folks from her area. It would make sense that she would go there, if needed, but it was a tough decision for all of us. That was also where my father died.

I talked about moving Mum to assisted living near Lori and me in Annapolis when the time finally came. I was still working but was available to visit every day, even a few times daily, and to bring her to our house for dinner and to the beach house on weekends. I believed I was thinking of my mother's happiness and welfare, but maybe I was thinking more about myself. I wanted it to be easier to see her more often, and I thought it would give my sister a break. Marge did not want a break.

What I did not immediately consider was everyone who was close to Mum in Pennsylvania, nor what my mother wanted. Mum would have missed her friends, her church (which she was driven to every Sunday), and all the visitors who were able to visit her in Pennsylvania. My sister visited her several times each week, did her laundry, and took her out to dinners. My cousin Josie had developed a deep and close relationship with my mother and would continue to visit her often at William Penn.

Sadly, my mother agreed that a move to William Penn might be a good decision for her. In preparation for the move, Lori, my sister, and I helped Mum go through all her belongings and we sorted them into "keep, Goodwill, or toss" piles and bags. That ended up being a difficult weekend, and Mum got upset at some things we thought were inconsequential.

To my mother, there were some areas, small or large, where she needed to maintain control of herself and her belongings. For instance, she couldn't find her favorite coffee scoop and I was blamed for throwing it away. I do not believe I did, but I apologized anyway, searched through each box and bag we had filled, and finally offered to get her a new one. She was not going to be permitted to make coffee at William Penn anyway, so it seemed very unimportant to me. It was important to Mum, and strangely, that coffee scoop is in my home now. Lori was blamed for losing the cord to the electric frying pan. Mum had always kept it neatly folded and threaded into a paper towel roll and it was gone. Lori never saw it but she also apologized anyway.

Mum moved to assisted living on September 1, 2013. Three weeks after her shift to William Penn, my sister and brother-in-law packed her in their car and brought her to Annapolis for Lori's and my wedding. Mum stayed with my sister at my niece's house for that weekend. I know it was not the most convenient for them and we did not get to see as much of my mother as I wanted. However, we could not have Mum stay at our house during our wedding preparation. I knew I could not give my mother the assistance she would need getting dressed and out the door for the wedding. So, once again, my sister stepped up and took care of Mum, helping immensely with our wonderful day.

We had rooms at a close-by hotel for Lori's mother and sister and many of my relatives. My brother and his fiancée were the only guests to stay with us. They stayed in the lower level where they had apartment-like privacy, and they helped with many of the last-minute details of the wedding. Everyone enjoyed the celebration of our nuptials, and I watched my mother closely. Mum smiled and laughed all evening and even "chair danced" with friends and family. I know she was genuinely happy for Lori and me and was relieved that I would no longer be alone. Mum told me that was her greatest worry about my lifestyle. At age ninety-eight, my mother could finally relax and stop worrying about her youngest child.

I never imagined, first, that I would have a wedding at all but especially that my entire extended family, many close friends, and the family of the woman I chose as my lifelong partner would surround me. It just was not supposed to be in the cards for me, but there we were and what fun we had! The only thing missing was Dad.

Our Perfect Day–September 21, 2013

After our wedding, Lori and I took a honeymoon cruise from Venice to Athens with several stops along the way, including Croatia. We chose Olivia, a gay cruise line, because the world did then and still does hold onto bigotry and bias. Of all the times in our lives, for those magical two weeks, we wanted to be comfortable and accepted as a married couple. We saw some of the world's most beautiful scenery and ate delicious and lavish Italian and Greek delicacies along the way. Every day was an extravaganza of delectable food, onboard entertainment, shore excursions at each port-of-call, and total acceptance. Our emotions ranged from sadness about leaving the ship and its atmosphere to excitement about getting back to our wonderful country and home, even with the difficulties and systemic bias that still exists.

Once we were home and settled again in our wonderful home, I checked in with my mother regularly. I say that now, but I know and I knew then that I could have called more. We talked on the phone before every Steeler game, just to make sure she did not forget to watch. Then I would call at halftime and at the end of the game. Hopefully, there was a celebration to share or we would complain about the mistakes that were made.

Mum was a huge fan of running back Jerome Bettis. His nickname was "the bus" and that is how she referred to him, even when she had the special and memorable opportunity to talk to him at Pittsburgh International Airport. When he learned that the little lady in the wheelchair nearby was a fan, he did not hesitate but went directly to her, shook her hand, and seemed as pleased to meet her as she was to be up close and personal with him.

I was always so happy, and slightly surprised, when my mother talked about all the visitors she had at William Penn. When my cousins, Jack and Barb, came from Boston to visit Barb's family in Pittsburgh, they always drove out to Level Green to see my mother and they continued even when she was in assisted living. My cousins, Jeff and Lisa, stopped in on Sunset Drive to visit, and then continued to take their children to see Mum no matter where she was. My nephew, Chad, flew in from his Air Force assignment in Utah to take his wife and their son to visit Marcus' great grandmother. Mum was special to everyone she knew. Even Marcus, who was only three years old when she died, later said that he missed his Grand Nan. I will help him hold the memory of her forever.

Lori and I visited often, but never often enough. We always played scrabble on the outside deck and took her to the Hot Rod Lounge Steak and Spaghetti House where we all had their salmon and pasta. My mother laughed so hard when Lori and I marveled at the huge pour of wine we were served at that restaurant. The glasses were the old style with the shorter and thicker stems but at five dollars a glass, who cared?

During one of the visits to the Hot Rod Lounge, Mum's walker got away from me while we helped Mum into the car. It rolled into the fast lane of Route 22. Do not worry; Mum was in the car. The traffic was very polite and let me scurry out to retrieve the three-wheeled contraption without incident. My mother was always so amused at the things that would happen when she was with Lori and me. Gradually Mum replaced the walker with a wheelchair that she remained in most of the time.

During the two years she lived at William Penn Care Center, I do not remember my mother ever introducing Lori as my wife. She never mentioned our relationship and, as far as I know, her friends never asked. I guessed that they assumed we were sisters or they just forgot to ask or care. They all forgot most things. At ninety-eight years old, my mother deserved to handle her introductions any way she chose. If she was still embarrassed that I was a lesbian, I was able to let it slide and I was never hurt. Knowing her, she probably did not even think of it, but just treated Lori like her own daughter. I do not think there was much that could have embarrassed my mother at that point. She was just proud of her family and delighted when we were with her. That is all I ever wanted.

Mum had a few falls in her room that gave her many bruises, including a black eye caused by falling while wearing her glasses. Those bruises made her look like she was wearing goggles because they perfectly showed the outline of her glass frames. She laughed at herself and said how ridiculous she looked. We tried to laugh with her but I just cried when I saw her. She looked so little and frail and all I wanted to do was take care of her. My sister met her at the hospital several times, and I was always on call and ready to drive at a moment's notice, but my sister never asked me to do that. She wanted me to wait until it was really serious and I was actually needed. Again, I should have made a better decision about driving up there every time.

Except for high blood pressure and arthritis that often gave Mum excruciating neck and shoulder pain, her health was good. As it happens for many senior citizens, one of her falls resulted in a broken hip. Mum was taken to the hospital after the fall and stayed there for several days. At ninety-eight years old, the doctor told us that Mum was too old to have surgery. Since she was wheelchair-bound anyway, the doctor recommended managing the pain and changing her position often enough so that slow healing could occur.

After that fall, I drove to Pittsburgh early Saturday morning, August 29th, arrived at my sister's house, and dropped my bags before heading to Forbes Regional Hospital to visit Mum. I spent most of Saturday through Tuesday at her side while we talked, laughed, and read the newspaper together. Of course, we played Scrabble. My mother was sharp until her final day. If she didn't beat me at Scrabble, she was always close. And I never let her win–she would have hated that. I will always keep that last score sheet from our game on September 1, 2015. All the discomfort about my sexuality was gone. My mother loved Lori and Lori loved her. There is nothing better than when you realize those you love most also love each other.

Driving away from the hospital and returning to my life in Annapolis was one of the hardest things I ever had to do, but Lori and I had to attend her nephew's wedding the following weekend. I planned on going back to see Mum on the weekend of September 12th but that plan was changed when I received the phone call from my sister the evening of September 9th. I can relive that minute in great detail and I cry all over again. Mum died quietly and alone, sitting in her wheelchair in her room. I will always go over in my mind what should or could have happened. Why wasn't I there? Why did I choose the wedding instead of staying with my mother? Again, Lori would have understood and agreed. Why didn't I bring her to live with Lori and me for her last year or two? I could go on and on.

I do know that my mother talked to Jesus and to my father every night. There were a few times when Mum believed she saw my dad at William Penn. She told us that she looked for him around the campus but could not find him. Mum missed my dad so much and one day stated that she wanted to be with him in heaven. She never said she was ready to die, but she was very practical about death and serious about her faith. Her time would come, but she was in no hurry nor was she afraid. Mum made the best of every minute she had on this planet. If I learned anything from her, I hope it was to make every minute count and also to try to remove anger, regret, resentment, guilt, blame, and worry from your life. Most of all, forgive. Forgive everybody, including myself.

The night before my mother's funeral, Lori and I stayed at a Red Roof Inn. It was far from fancy but, as my mother would say, "At least it was clean." It was the closest to Sunset Drive, and there was no room at my sister's or at any of my cousins' houses. Friends and relatives came from Oregon, Maryland, Ohio, Massachusetts, California, and all over Pennsylvania. We needed Mum and Dad's house to congregate in that night. It would have felt right, all of us gathering around the dining room table and dragging chairs from all over the house, like we had done for so many years. But it is funny that, on the other hand, I am glad we were not at a place where so many memories had been made and where I could see every chair my parents sat on and every item they touched.

You never know what you really want until you try it and then make your decision. So, if the decision is that you really did not want it, it is too late. Now I am happy that I only saw my mother alive. I only saw her with the vitality she maintained her entire life. I never needed to search her face for a sign of recognition, see her chest raise and lower with her last breath, or have a moment when she did not know me. But at the same time, I also wish I had been with her when she slipped away. You just cannot have it both ways.

I am proud and satisfied that I spoke at her funeral. I never would have believed that I could do that, but only the minister had spoken at my father's funeral and I always wondered why. With my mother sitting at Dad's service, it would have been too devastating to look at her and try to get words to actually come out of my mouth. This time, I cared so much that each person in attendance would have some reminders of how special she was and would understand how appreciative we were that they were there in her honor. I just spoke from my heart and stole a few items from a list of ninety memories and attributes I had written as a gift for her ninetieth birthday. I titled it "Some of the Things That Make You the BEST Mother in The Whole World!!" Many in the congregation were glad that I spoke, and my siblings were happy they did not.

At my mother's funeral, my cousin, Jack, noticed that all three of her children told him, in separate conversations, that he or she was Mum's favorite. Jack knew we were joking (in a way) but he understood that we were each made to feel so special that we really did believe each was her favorite. If a parent is so loving, caring, and attentive that each child believes himself to be the favorite, that must be optimal parenting and another great lesson from my mother.

In the absence of parents, I felt orphaned, and my age did not matter. Who is left to call? Who loves you unconditionally? No one. That's fine, because I expect conditions to be placed on all my other relationships, but it feels awful to have the unconditional love gone. I fought for so many years for my life to change, to be different, to be better, to be understood, and to be loved in my own truth, but suddenly, I wanted life to continue as it had always been. I still had a longing to proclaim my specialness to two people who were no longer there. That, of course, was impossible.

I believe my siblings were fighting to have Mum and Dad back too—to turn back the clock. Our parents had gone missing and there is hopelessness in that feeling. Soon you just have to move on, and those silly thoughts have to be kept inside until they fade, and maybe someday, dissipate completely. There was no fight for respect or equality between my brother, sister, and me, but possibly a struggle to be known in a new way. We had always only known each other with respect to our relationship with our parents. Now we are on our own to determine what we are as orphaned siblings.

It was good that Mum and Dad's house had been sold and my parent's belongings had been divided or claimed a few years earlier. I do not think we could have managed to go back in the house without Mum or Dad with us, not me anyway. My brother, sister, and I prided ourselves on the civility we practiced when our parents were gone. There were probably some unspoken disagreements or tension regarding who got or who deserved what, but it was never important enough to mention. Our parents had taught us well by being the wonderful role models they were. All they ever wanted from us was our time and I hope we gave enough. I know my siblings did and I know I did not.

Janis E. Mills

chapter thirteen

LIFE'S THIRD ACT/WHO AM I ON MY WAY TO BECOMING?

FOR MY SIXTY-FIFTH BIRTHDAY, Lori and I invited friends and colleagues to celebrate with us at Brio Italian restaurant in Annapolis. Smart, funny, and kind friends have filled my life, and I was touched that those closest to me drove from Delaware and Pennsylvania for the party. Even though it was December and the middle of a school year, a few wise coworkers suspected that the gathering was my way of throwing myself a retirement party six months premature. They were right. The dual-purpose party was meant to replace a typical retirement dinner where guests pay for their own meals and contribute to a gift. I did it my way.

I was amid a "lifes is too short" epiphany. Being a lesbian was no longer a worry and there was no one who would be embarrassed by my gayness. Work started to feel unimportant and, even though I had been an educator for forty-two years, I wanted to do more, and I thought I could be a better person if I stopped working. I wanted to volunteer, learn new things, or just start living differently. I wanted to pick up where my mother left off, but it did not take long to admit to myself that no one could ever do that. It was wishful thinking that I could be the one to emulate her and to be loved like she was loved. I will never be what my vision of her is but what I can do is try harder than ever to be the best me that I can be.

In her book, *My Life So Far*, Jane Fonda called the third act of her life, her final thirty years, "Beginnings." She said that is what it feels like. I agree. I felt like I could start a new kind of life for my final thirty years. Since my father and mother lived to be ninety-four and ninety-eight respectively, I believe the odds of me making it to one hundred years old are pretty good. I am not sure I want to live that long, but as long as I feel good and can take care of the necessities myself, that would be okay. Of course, I want to look passable, too, and I hope Lori still wants to go out to dinner and to the theatre with me.

I have finally started learning from all the wounds I have and mistakes I made, both the self-inflicted and those I imposed on others. When Jane Fonda wrote about the third act of her life, she inspired me to make sure mine is on track to make it full of significant differences I can make within myself and for others. I want an ending that is amazing on earth as opposed to in the afterlife.

Telling the story of my life took a lot of remembering, some very painful and some I would like to change. I cannot compromise myself because I am all I have. I thought I was just living out this story, but I now realize that I am actually in charge of this story. I want to know who I am on my way to becoming. I want life-altering experiences that happen during my final thirty years. I still need to see Niagara Falls and Mount Rushmore and I need to go to Paris with Lori. We can hold hands in public.

Exploring my creativity by learning to write has been one piece of my "Beginnings." Lori and I are trying to find a new spiritual path and I am starting to give my time to others. I saw something new in myself when the Covid-19 pandemic hit. One of the most important times of my "shelter at home" days was making masks for our local hospital. When I made my plan for the day, I always made a list; it was so much fun to see writing and sewing on that agenda.

I refuse to ever blame anything on age or to stop doing something only because of my age. My interests do change, perhaps because of age or at least the effects of aging, but as long as I am physically able, I will push myself to continue learning and building physical and mental muscle. I do need to stop yearning to turn back the clock, not to be younger or to look better but to have "do overs." They are gone so I just need to get over it.

I like Jane Fonda's idea to "finish the task of finishing ourselves" and to further develop our wisdom, wholeness, and authenticity. I am transforming my expectation of old age and I am enjoying aging with freedom. After all, I was a first-time bride at age sixty-two. Being totally at peace with myself and comfortable in the skin I own, life is so much easier and more pleasant than all the years of hiding and lying. Now I am doing my best to appreciate what my past has taught me, and I am trying to make those lessons part of my future. I want an uplifting, redemptive end to my story, beyond just the fact that I survived.

The scared little eight-year-old girl who was afraid to say, "That's me," when my mother defined queer is now the brave, married woman who is not afraid to say, "This is my wife."

***

I was seventy years old on my last birthday and I am at a new beginning, in a new phase of life. I no longer have the responsibilities of a high school principal or of a daughter. I am allowed to think differently and to be myself. Intelligent, inspiring, powerful, and experienced women, Michelle Obama, Jane Fonda, and Jill Biden, just to name a few, believe they are still in progress. I do not mean to compare myself to them, but I do hope I will always be evolving and learning also.

I have had many different goals and aims over my lifetime. I thought everything would be wonderful if my parents only knew I was gay. Now the price is that they are gone.

I became a wife and continue to adapt to that role, learning what it is like to truly love and make a life with another person. Though many of my jobs were positions of power and we all have moments when we feel unimportant and unheard, I kept those few moments to myself—of course I did—because I knew it was important to demonstrate confidence without arrogance while I was an instructional leader. Fortunately, those times were rare, so I always focused on the work ahead and the learning that was still ahead. I continue to do that.

The early years were about change, later about stability. I am not looking for acceptance or validation but the specific life episodes I have shared illustrate truths about the self. I waited too long to appreciate my strength. I did not know my power and I regret not coming out to my parents when I was very young but I did not trust what their reaction would be and I was frozen in the fear of being cast out. It was my choice to stay away, not call often enough, and not tell the truth about my life.

They were not trying to pry; they just wanted to be part of my life and wanted to know how their youngest was doing. That included what she was doing. I was too afraid to tell them. Now I realize how sad that must have made my mother and father. After all, I lived almost three hundred fifty miles away, so I maintained the attitude of "What difference did it make?" Well, it made a big difference to them. I feel lucky that they were mine.

It was fortunate for me that I spent so many years working with children. I still watch the kids in my family and my neighborhood as they approach every day believing in the goodness of mankind. They help me keep a positive attitude about whatever frightens me in this world. I do believe we will be okay. Our country will emerge from the four years with our last president and the Covid-19 pandemic more united and more hopeful. We must all stick together and strengthen the bonds between all racial, ethnic, religious, gender, and LGBTQ groups. Anyone who has been persecuted knows how important it is to work together to overcome all racism, bigotry, persecution, and bias.

My story has a happy ending, but I do not want to make it sound like I believe the lives of all LGBTQ+ people are finally trouble-free. Though my life is much easier than it was in all previous decades and gays are, by far, more accepted, maybe even understood, there remains a struggle and we are well-aware that we are different.

Our transgender brothers and sisters deal with harassment, self-loathing, abuse, and the threat of violence every day. No one can tell a gay person is a homosexual just by looks but most other groups that experience hatred can be spotted by the color of their skin, religious garb, accents, or their size eighteen pumps, deep voices, and large, masculine hands. Not long ago, a transgender woman was brutally stabbed in a targeted attack at MacArthur Park in Los Angeles simply because she is trans.

Hate crimes still exist, but thanks to Barack Obama, they have a label and a law. As briefly mentioned earlier, the Matthew Shepherd and James Byrd Jr. Hate Crimes Protection Act was an act of Congress that President Obama signed into law on October 28, 2009. Race, color, gender, sexual orientation, and national origin are motives for the commission of crimes. Every person who looks different from you is exactly the same as you and every one of your family members. Each person is loved by someone, part of a family, and equal in every way. All oppressed groups hurt when racism, bigotry, prejudice, or persecution exist. So, reader, please be a part of the solution.

I am the culmination of all the lessons I have learned from each person who has touched my life. I hope I have chosen the best parts of each lesson and wrapped them into the individual I am today. To have relationships, we tell little pieces of our story. So, some version of a life story exists with each person. No one gets every puzzle piece. This story is not my imagination; it is my experiences working through life as a gay girl. Those are the only two sources of material I have. Sometimes when you tell the ugly and painful parts of life, the world opens itself to you, so this is my way of making sense of the world around me.

Again, like Michelle Obama, I am an "ordinary person who found herself on an extraordinary journey." Of course, her journey was unique and mine was not. That is why I wrote, hoping that sharing would help many who are in similar situations that I was. Much of my journey I took alone, but I came out okay. I finally allowed myself to be known and now to be heard. I hope I have made others feel that it is important to share their stories too. The quotation I recently heard from "The Boys in the Band" states, "Show me a happy homosexual and I'll show you a gay corpse." My deepest wish is that there is not one homosexual on the planet that believes that. The play, and movie, is a story of gay life in the 1970s when, from the outside, gay life seemed to be a series of parties, rallies, and drug and alcohol-laden free love, but it was also a desperate time of self-hate.

***

I do have some advice for parents:

Love, listen, accept. "Reject the notion that children are disposable if they are not mini versions of you. Guiding a child to be a loving and compassionate global citizen should be a parent's goal." I heard Gabrielle Union say that and I think it is perfect. Allow your children to be who they are by loving and supporting them.

***

For someone struggling to come out:

You will have a life of joy–some hardships–some bumps in the road. Love yourself and persevere. Nothing is wrong with a life if it is spent with the person you love. When you think about the side effects of coming out, do not only think about the possible losses (family, friends, employment) but focus on the positive effects of honesty, living your truth, and the elimination of the anxiety that comes with the lying and hiding.

ACKNOWLEDGMENTS

WRITING THIS BOOK WAS far more difficult than I ever imagined it would be. What could be so hard about telling my true story? The mistakes, the embarrassments, and the secrets are not what I am proud of but, overall, I am proud of how I prevailed through the challenges and of my hard-earned accomplishments. Sharing the difficulties was important if it can help others who are climbing similar hurdles in their quests to reveal their truths.

I want to start by thanking my extraordinary wife, Lori, for tolerating my incessant disappearances into our loft and my nonstop talking, thinking, and even dreaming about ideas that should or should not be included in my book. She kept a level head and waited until the end to read because she wanted to be sure that this is my story and not one she influenced or changed. Lori listened to every frustration I faced and realigned my thinking when it needed to be straightened. My lifelong partner makes both the journey and destination worthwhile.

I owe an enormous debt of gratitude to Iris Krasnow, New York Times Best Selling author and Senior Editor of AARP's *The Ethel*. The role Iris played during this rewarding, but arduous project cannot be simply stated. She was my mentor, coach, line editor, friend, and therapist. Iris believed in my story before we ever met in person. She pushed me to be brave, clear, and detailed with her relentless questioning that forced me to dig deeper. Her challenge to me was to show you, not tell you, my story by painting a picture through detailed descriptions. After only five months of working together in person, Covid-19 forced us to work remotely, which changed our dynamic and banter enormously. But still, her bolstering words, some in the form of one-word texts, arrived at precisely the right moments. Iris convinced me that my life has been interesting, colorful, and worth telling. I hope you agree.

To my siblings, Maggie and Bob, I love you so much and appreciate your perspectives on historical family details and on how you saw my life unfolding. I can always count on your honesty, and I especially love it when it is complimentary to my work. You have been there for me my entire life and thinking back through the years while writing this was a wonderful reminder of all the times I depended on my big brother and sister who never disappointed. Bob and Maggie were also kind enough to allow me to share private details from their pasts that became part of my story.

Special thanks to Sherry Surratt, who continues to play an important role in my life and was helpful both with clarifying memories and with her artistic eye when it came to choosing photographs and discussing ideas for the cover. Melisa Steffens, a neighbor turned friend, expressed a desire to read my creation as soon as she learned about my work. Sherry and Melisa wrote detailed and constructive comments and gave freely of their time to discuss nuances of the text. They pushed me to clarify concepts, explore further, and explain deeper. Each of them enjoyed my book, felt the emotional ups and downs I experienced, and could relate to personal situations, as well as see how helpful *Coming Out: It Only Took Fifty Years* could be to individuals or families experiencing their own coming out stories.

For the first time in my life, I get to thank a publisher. My gratitude goes to Lee Fitzsimmons of Desert Palm Press for accepting my work and believing its value is worthy of print. Lee encouraged me to further develop my secondary characters so you would see my story and not simply read about it. Lee aligned me with my wonderful editor, Kaycee Hawn, who painstakingly studied every detail and polished my work into the final product I hope you have enjoyed. Kaycee is the first person to allow me to reach my goal of inspiring others to share their own truths and for that I am forever grateful. That made me love and appreciate my story more than I ever have.

I want to explain some things that happened while writing the truth about my own life. Memories are imperfect and some details are not appropriate to include. I have shared, to the best of my knowledge, but I have changed identities of some of the players because they might not remember their involvement in my life exactly as I remember them. Some of the women who shared special times with me are straight and living straight lives with husbands and children. I do not want any of their family members to learn anything from me that those women would not or have not shared. In Chapter Nine, *Courting Straight Girls,* I combined characters and created amalgams so they would not be recognized. No one person is exactly how she is portrayed, and names and unimportant details have been changed to make each one unrecognizable. The information was changed for their protection and mine. I just don't want to piss anybody off too much. So, if you think you recognize anyone, you do not.

ABOUT JANIS E. MILLS, PHD

Jan Mills was born in Pittsburgh, Pennsylvania. She earned a Bachelor of Science in Special Education and a Master of Education from Indiana University of Pennsylvania. She taught special education and high school mathematics for fifteen years in Prince George's County, Maryland.

After earning certification in Administration and Supervision from the University of Maryland, she served sixteen years as a secondary school administrator, ten of which were high school principal in Prince George's and Montgomery Counties, both in Maryland. She earned her PhD in Instructional Leadership for a Changing Population at Notre Dame of Maryland University in Baltimore and taught Educational Leadership as an Adjunct Professor at McDaniel College in Westminster, Maryland. After retirement, Dr. Mills remains active in the Anne Arundel County Public Schools as a mentor to new principals and assistant principals.

Jan contributes to her community through her volunteer work at the Maryland Therapeutic Riding Center and at the Anne Arundel County Medical Center.

Connect with Janis …

Email: jemaddierose@comcast.net
Facebook: https://www.facebook.com/janis.mills.140

Note to Readers:

Thank you for reading a book from Desert Palm Press. We appreciate you as a reader and want to ensure you enjoy the reading process. We would like you to consider posting a review on your preferred media sites and/or your blog or website.

For more information on upcoming releases, author interviews, contest, giveaways and more, please sign up for our newsletter and visit us as at Desert Palm Press: www.desertpalmpress.com and "Like" us on Facebook: Desert Palm Press.

Bright Blessings

www.ingramcontent.com/pod-product-compliance
Lightning Source LLC
Chambersburg PA
CBHW060310130626
46546CB00015B/916